Be A pineapple

Build a Life

BK

T0048440

BRILL KID
The BIG number

2

yummy!

life's like a
SANDWICH!

AWESOMENESS-
THE NEXT LEVEL

Grannies
+ Jam =
Happiness

JAM

Andy Cope, Gavin Oattes & Will Hussey

brought to life by Amy Bradley

'My mum Sellotaped my eyelids open and made me read this book because she said it'd do me good. Thank you mum. It's made me super-positive but I now need glasses.'
Renne Specsaver (age 10) from Wimbledon

'I keep this book in the bathroom so my family can read it while they're pooing. Unfortunately, just last week, I dropped it in the toilet. But not to worry, I fished it out and used my mum's hair dryer to dry the pages. All good.'
Mel Bourne (Jnr) (age 8) from Melbourne

'I read Brill Kid Volume 1. It was much better than this. So if you haven't read that yet, please buy them both.'
Will Hussey (age 43) author, from Bookingham

'I really like this book but the pages are crinkly and it smells funny.'
Mrs Bourne (age 31) from Melbourne

'I gave this book to my brother for Christmas and, guess what, he shrugged and said he preferred computer games to... and I quote... 'stupid old books'. So I read it instead. Now my life is stellar and his is rubbish. Thank you, authors.'
Mustafa Selfie (age 14) from Ho Chi Min City

'Brill Kid 2 is exactly like Toy Story 2. Except it's a book instead of an animation and it's not about a bunch of toys who come alive and join together to have an adventure. It also doesn't have Woody or Mr Potato-head or Slinky or any of the characters. So actually this book is nothing like Toy Story 2. What I mean is that Toy Story 1 was really good, but Toy Story 2 was even better. I'm still not sure that's clear?'
Errol Sequel (age 7) from Florida

This book is so funny I've accidentally let out a bit of wee.'
Esmerelda Littletinkle (age 8) from London-on-Thames

'It says "the big number 2" on the front cover. I like that you've let the authors make a poo joke before we even begin. Thank you, publishers.'
Ivor Flusher (age 11) from Glasgow

'I see that one of the authors is listed as "Gavin Oattes". I think you've spelt "Oats" wrong. Just saying.'
Nathaniel Oats (age 4) from Kilmarnock-on-Thames

'I've not read it yet but it sure looks great.'
Hermione Procrastinator (age 2) from Swindon-on-Sea

'This is an amazing book. 'Brilliant Kid' is such a great idea. Such a shame that that Jeff bloke copied your idea and wrote his own "Wimpy Kid" series. He did movies too. I bet you're well jell. Have you sued him yet?'
Sue Judge (age 13) from Hampton Court

'Hang on a sec. At first glance it seems like there are three authors who are all boys, and one illustrator who is a girl. That's sexist. Surely there should be three female illustrators or it's not fair.'
Esme Equality (age 15) from Geneva

'Someone once told me that dinosaurs didn't read and now look at them. They're extinct! So this book could literally save your life. Read it TODAY before it's too late.'
Matthew Triceratops (age 16) from Wrexham

'There's a town called "Reading". I actually live there. It's spelt "reading" as in what you do with a book and yet it's pronounced "Redding". It's the same kind of thing with "scones". It's no wonder us kids get confused. Plus, you'd think that there'd be lots of people reading in Reading, but to the naked eye, it seems pretty much like everywhere else.'
Mo Headscratcher (age 7) from Reading

'Diary of a Brilliant Kid volume 1 was the best thing since sliced bread. Diary of a Brilliant Kid volume 2 is even better. That makes it better than whatever the best thing was before sliced bread was invented, but I'm not sure what that was? I'm guessing unsliced bread, but it could be buns or pitta bread or some-thing? Or maybe the wheel or fire even? Does anybody know?'
Hovis Warburton IV (age 11) from Yorkshire

This edition first published 2022.

*Registered office*
John Wiley & Sons Ltd, The Atrium, Southern Gate, Chichester, West Sussex, PO19 8SQ, United Kingdom

For details of our global editorial offices, for customer services and for information about how to apply for permission to reuse the copyright material in this book please see our website at www.wiley.com.

*Library of Congress Cataloging-in-Publication Data*

A catalogue record for this book is available from the British Library.

ISBN 9780857088918 (paperback) ISBN 9780857088970 (ePDF)

Cover design/image: Amy Bradley

Printed and bound in Great Britain by Bell and Bain Ltd, Glasgow

To every kid on the planet – thank you for being you. You are amazing. You are incredible. But you're not perfect.

Good news; neither is anyone else!

This book will ease the pressures of life by reminding you to quit trying to be perfect and start being remarkable. It's not about trying to be the best in the world, it's about being the best FOR the world.

We wrote Brill Kid 2 to nudge you in the right direction.

Thank you from Amy, Will, Gav, and Andy xxxx

# Running Order:

# Running Order:

Meat
REAL
deal!!

# dollop one:

## You are the ~~meat~~ REAL deal

4

Silliness Scale

Pop yourself on to YouTube and search the following...
'Goat eating a Dorito'. And watch it at least 42 times.

Why? Because it's a goat eating a Dorito and it's silly.
And hilarious.

PLOT SPOILER ALERT: at Brill Kid HQ we love silliness.
We also love facts btw...

A small child could swim through the
veins of a blue whale.

That's a smart fact but a really bad idea.

But we also appreciate that this is a learning book. It
has important messages about happiness, wellbeing,

resilience and life, all of which are serious. Which is exactly why we'll sometimes throw some silliness your way. This time it was a Dorito-eating goat, but later on we've got the story of the Three Little Pigs like you've never heard before. We've got a bunch of grannies who have changed the world, Joe's Amazing Technicolour Wheelie-Bin and the word 'hippopottomonstrosesquipedaliophobia'.

When you get to these bits PLEASE NOTE, they're not silly by accident. We've carefully crafted these pages to be deliberately silly.

Because silliness makes you learn faster.

Silliness Scale

↑ Looks like this!

That's why we've just this moment made a decision to put a 'silliness rating' next to the really stupid bits. That way, if your mum or dad is reading this book to you at bedtime, and they're expecting it to be full of learning, they can skip the really silly bits and just cover the serious stuff. Parents like serious stuff and we want to keep them happy. But when they've gone, you can switch the light back on and read the silly bits to yourself.

Here's our silliness scale.

1: Good solid content with no silliness at all (aka, 'boring').

2: Still mostly un-silly, but a bit sillier than 1 (aka, 'still a bit boring').

3: Contains mild silliness.

4: Expect some randomness.

5: Getting really rather idiotic.

6: A bit sillier than 5. Occasionally stupid.

7: Warning; things will be getting very silly indeed!

8: A bit like 7, but with probable bottom jokes too.

9: Seriously silly with big dollops of stupidity.

10: Ridiculous! Nonsensical. If you're a serious kid, look away now.

Oh, and btw, there are no 1s or 2s. The bit you've just read is a 3. Fasten your seatbelt, young reader. Things are going to get waaaaaaaay sillier.

# THANK YOU.

'Begin at the beginning,' the King said, very gravely, 'and go on till you come to the end: then stop.'

(From Alice in Wonderland by Lewis Carroll)

# Our Story Starter

With our silliness explanation out of the way we can move on to the actual book itself. This is the ribbon cutting bit.

OPEN

We do declare Brill Kid 2 to be officially open. We really hope you enjoy it. It's called 'The Big Number 2' for two very obvious reasons; it's the second in the series and it also allowed us to make a 'number 2' poo joke on the front cover. And in case you're wondering we are very proud of both these points, especially the toilet based 'number 2'.

Poo

But you see this book is not just a book full of poo references and silly stories. It is in fact an incredibly serious book jam-packed with life-changing, life-enhancing and life-fulfilling advice that, if followed correctly, will make you explode with awesomeness. Not literally of course, that would be both dangerous and messy. If you exploded in the kitchen your parents would be wiping bits of you off the walls and ceiling for weeks to come. And even after they thought they'd cleaned you all up, in a month or two they'd find, say, a finger or some intestines behind the fridge.

We wanted to start the book by talking about something really important. But where do we start because *life* is really important, every day is really important and YOU are really important. Most books of this kind will start with topics such as 'confidence' or the 'human brain' or 'anxiety' or by telling you it's 'okay to not be okay'. Of course, all of these are perfectly reasonable ways to start a book. But if you were wanting to raise the bar on 'book openers' you'd have to come up with a theme that no other books in the history of books have ever started with.

So we chose – *ahem* – crisps.

yes, crisps-
BEST invention
ever!!!

We all love crisps, don't we? Crisps are great, possibly one of the best snacks ever invented. In fact, they may well be one of the best inventions ever invented. This got us thinking about who invented 'inventions', which led us to agree that the best thing since sliced bread is, in actual fact, sliced potato. The invention of crisps is right up there with fire, games consoles and spaghetti hoops.

Crisps are so yummy and yet so versatile. You can have them on their own, in a sandwich, dipped in salsa, floating in your coke or sprinkled on other crisps. We know crisps aren't healthy but we're starting with them because we all know there's one thing about crisps that blows minds every day all across the world. We all know there's one thing about this delicious fried potato snack that creates excitement like no other potato-based food.

That's right, young ladies and gents, the moment that you reach into a bag of crisps and pull from it a crisp the size of your face. Yup, we don't need to tell you how magical this moment is. A crisp the size of your face is truly one of life's epic moments. So much so that we instantly turn to every other person in the room and show it off. Or we take pictures and send it to our friends as if we've won the lottery.

It's probably fair to say there are not many things in life to rival this level of enthusiasm. Birthdays? Maybe. But the thing about birthdays is they're predictable. All you've got to do is survive for another 365 days and your birthday will roll around again. Same day every year. I mean, how dull is that?

But pulling a ginormous crisp from a bag ... it's so random. You just never know. Which makes it super-exciting.

And that's what this book is all about. Reaching into Brill Kid (the 'Big Number 2', still funny, see!) and pulling from it something that gets you so excited it might just set your soul on fire. You might not pull from it what you were looking for or what you were expecting. And that's the exact point. It's all about reaching in, headfirst, feet off the ground and grabbing whatever's in here with two hands. Embracing the randomness. Making the best of whatever you pull from this crisp packet of a book.

So yeah, there you have it. This book is your big metaphorical bag of crisps. Now you've opened it, it's time to reach in, laugh, read, laugh, learn, laugh some more and get sharing!

# Life is a Sandwich

Hang on a sec. Didn't you just say life was a bag of crisps? Now you're suggesting it's a bread-based snack? This book seems to be turning into some sort of meal deal. Come on, authors, explain yourselves. Life; is it crisps or a sandwich?

Well, tbh, we were suggesting *this book* is like a bag of crisps. *Life* is, in fact, a sandwich! Lettuce explain … Lettuce? Sandwiches? Anyone?

Firstly, sandwiches are delicious. Unless you put something in it that's disgusting, then it's just disgusting, and you don't want the sandwich anymore. Sometimes a sandwich is so yummy, you want more and more until you are full up on the yumminess that is your sandwich. Especially when they're cut into triangles, right? We can all agree right now that sandwiches taste better when cut into triangles, yeah? Good.

So, as you can see they're just like life. Some would argue that it's all about the bread but in the sandwich of life, the tasty bit is the filling. Life is sandwiched between a slice of birth and a slice of death. The middle bit ... that's where the action is. The flavour.

The Sandwich of life:

In other words, you're born, you live and you die. You can't change the being born part and, in the interests of telling it as it is, nobody gets out alive.

# Fact-ivity

## Fact:

The inventor of the Frisbee was cremated and made into a Frisbee after he died.

*We like this idea* →

After he dies, Dr Andy wants to be made into a book. Will's going to be recycled into something that can be recycled so he can never actually be got rid of. Gav wants to be baked into a cake. And illustrator Amy wants to be made into a set of crayons.

BRILL KID

↑ Andy

← Will

Gav

↑ Amy

## Activity:

And your good self?
What do you want to be recycled as?

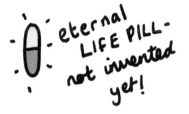
- eternal
LIFE PILL -
not invented
yet!

So, being born is guaranteed. Way into the distance, unless someone invents an eternal life pill (which they actually might), death is pretty much nailed on. But the middle bit is up for grabs. The filling is life itself. And truly living life to the full is not always guaranteed or definite. We all like different fillings but the most exciting part is you get to choose your own. Over time you begin to understand what you like, what works for you, what you want more of and what makes you want to puke.

You get a little more daring and adventurous with your filling and sometimes all we want is 'just ham' or 'just cheese', which is fine if you want a dull sandwich. But if life's a sandwich - *and you're the sandwich maker* - why not fill it with epic ingredients. How about a 'Grilled-Cheese-Sloppy-Joe-Melter-Subwoofing-Haggis-Special-Scooby-Snack-Yum-Rockets'. That's a special sandwich right there! It's a full sandwich. It's an exciting sandwich. It's a tasty sandwich. It's a unique sandwich. It's the best sandwich I can possibly imagine and I created it!

In fact, I'm going to have my Grilled-Cheese-Sloppy-Joe-Melter-Subwoofing-Haggis-Special-Scooby-Snack-Yum-Rockets *toasted.* With a side of face-sized crisps!

Here's the thing - you get to choose, most of the time.

We say 'most of the time' because we've all had moments when the sandwich is thrown down in front of us and it's full of stuff we don't like. But we're told, 'Get it eaten coz there's nothing else!' You'll have days like that. Days when you just need to suck it up.

But this book is about making sure most days are epic, with an occasional bad one thrown in, rather than most days being bad, with an occasional epic one thrown in.

Heck, what we're trying to say is that it's your life and therefore YOUR SANDWICH! You are the sandwich maker.

If your sandwich is rubbish, or not exciting enough, or full of cucumber, why not start experimenting? Adjust the filling, try something new, discover new flavours, drop the bland, upgrade the ingredients.

This book is a bag of crisps

a yummy life Sandwich

Still with us? It's fairly simple. This book is a bag of crisps that you can grab ideas from to help you make a yummy life sandwich. Oh, and we also want you to be the milk!

# Be the milk

Wait, what? *Be the milk?*

Yeah, *be* the milk.

But a page ago you were wanting me to be a packet of crisps, then you suggested I morphed into a something with cheese and pickle. What's this milk malarkey? Please try to keep up. The book is crisps and life is a sandwich. The milk. That's quite different. *You're* the milk. Obviously!

*I'm* the milk? How can I be the milk? The milk is the actual milk, surely. I've just checked and you've given this page a silliness rating of 4. It feels like a 7 at least. What do you mean, *I'm* the milk?

Imagine an empty bowl and you fill it with Rice Krispies. Just Rice Krispies, no milk yet, please don't get ahead of us here. Just Rice Krispies on their own, nothing else.

How would you describe them?

Plain. Still. Muted. Pale. Crispy. Dull. Dry. Bland. Parched. Basic. Thirsty. Dusty. Boring. Uneventful. Beige. They are simply not exciting. The Krispies are lifeless until you add the magic ingredient ...

The milk!

Then what happens?

They come alive. The little rascals rise. They Snap, Crackle and Pop ... they fizz, they bang, they whizz. They float! You can see them moving in the bowl in front of you, some even try to escape over the side.

The bowl is totally dull until you add the milk. Then things get exciting!

Think about life; childhood, school, maths, family, play time, watching TV, hobbies, history, relationships, playing Monopoly, learning French, walking in the drizzle, reading a book - everything is just one great big giant bowl of Rice Krispies.

These things exist in your life. They just need one magic ingredient to make them snap, crackle and pop. They need YOU. That makes YOU the milk.

# YOU are the magic ingredient!

Here's another horrible little truth that we're going to sneak in without anyone really noticing; there are a lot of people who have lives that haven't got very much snap, crackle or pop. Some people forget they're the milk. Plus, if you leave Rice Krispies in the bowl too long, they go mushy. They stop bouncing. If you have a look around at some of the adults, they've gone a bit, erm ... soggy. If you're not careful, life can become a little bit bland.

You've got to keep your bowl fresh.

Yes, *fresh milk* every day.

And remember, YOU are the milk. So YOU have to be refreshed every day. Otherwise your day will get soggy. So, to summarise our ribbon-cutting speech – this book is a bag of crisps, life is a sandwich but, most importantly, you are the one that can make things happen. You are the secret ingredient.

# BE THE MILK!

# dollop two:
## The parable of the okay day

### Silliness Scale
5

# 10 Facts about right now:

1. You're reading this right now.
2. You're realising that's a stupid fact.
4. You didn't notice we skipped number 3.
5. You're checking now.
6. You're smiling.
7. You're still reading this even though it's completely stupid.
9. You didn't notice we skipped number 8.
10. You're checking again and smiling that you fell for it again.
11. Despite being tricked twice, you're actually enjoying this.
12. This sentence contains exactly threee erors.[1]

[1] Two spelling mistakes, obviously! Plus the sentence only has two errors which is the third mistake.

An okay day, followed by an okay day, followed by an okay day, followed by an okay day, followed by an okay day, followed by an okay day, followed by an okay day means you've had seven okay days on the bounce.

Therefore, you've lived an *okay* week.

An okay week, followed by an okay week, followed by an okay week, followed by an okay week means you've lived an okay month.

An okay month, followed by an okay month, followed by an okay month, followed by an okay month, followed by an okay month, followed by an okay month, followed by an okay month, followed by an okay month, followed by an okay month, followed by an okay month, followed by an okay month, followed by an okay month means you've lived an *okay* year.

An okay year, followed by an okay year, followed by an okay year, followed by an okay year, followed by an okay year, followed by an okay year, followed by an okay year, followed by an okay year, followed by an okay year, followed by an okay year, followed by an okay year, followed by an okay year, followed by an okay year, followed by an okay year, followed by an okay year, followed by an okay year, followed by an okay year, followed by an okay year, followed by an okay year, followed by an okay year, followed by an okay year, followed by an okay year, followed by

an okay year, followed by an okay year, followed by
an okay year, followed by an okay year, followed by
an okay year, followed by an okay year, followed by an
okay year, followed by an okay year, followed by an okay
year, followed by an okay year, followed by an okay year,
followed by an okay year, followed by an okay year,
followed by an okay year, followed by an okay year,
followed by an okay year, followed by an okay year,
followed by an okay year, followed by an okay year,
followed by an okay year, followed by an okay year,
followed by an okay year, followed by an okay year,
followed by an okay year, followed by an okay year,
followed by an okay year, followed by an okay year,
followed by an okay year, followed by an okay year,
followed by an okay year, followed by an okay year,
followed by an okay year, followed by an okay year,
followed by an okay year, followed by an okay year,
followed by an okay year, followed by an okay year,
followed by an okay year, followed by an okay year,
followed by an okay year, followed by an okay year,
followed by an okay year, followed by an okay year,
followed by an okay year, followed by an okay year,
followed by an okay year, followed by an okay year,
followed by an okay year, followed by an okay year,
followed by an okay year, followed by an okay year,
followed by an okay year, followed by an okay year,
followed by an okay year, followed by an okay year,
followed by an okay year, followed by an okay year,
followed by an okay year, followed by an okay year,
followed by an okay year, followed by an okay year,
followed by an okay year, followed by an okay year,

followed by an okay year, followed by an okay year,
followed by an okay year, followed by an okay year,
followed by an okay year, followed by an okay year,
followed by an okay year, followed by an okay year,
followed by an okay year, followed by an okay year,
followed by an okay year, followed by an okay year,
followed by an okay year, followed by an okay year,
followed by an okay year, followed by an okay year,
followed by an okay year, followed by an okay year,
followed by an okay year, followed by an okay year,
followed by an okay year, followed by an okay year,
followed by an okay year, followed by an okay year,
followed by an okay year, followed by an okay year,
followed by an okay year, followed by an okay year,
followed by an okay year, followed by an okay year,
followed by an okay year, followed by an okay year,
followed by an okay year, followed by an okay year,
followed by an okay year, followed by an okay year,
followed by an okay year, followed by an okay year,
followed by an okay year, followed by an okay year,
followed by an okay year, followed by an okay year,
followed by an okay year, followed by an okay year,
followed by an okay year, followed by an okay year,
followed by an okay year, followed by an okay year,
followed by an okay year, followed by an okay year,
followed by an okay year, followed by an okay year,
followed by an okay year, followed by an okay year,
followed by an okay year, followed by an okay year,
followed by an okay year, followed by an okay year,
followed by an okay year, followed by an okay year,

followed by an okay year, followed by an okay year,
followed by an okay year, followed by an okay year,
followed by an okay year, followed by an okay year,
followed by an okay year, followed by an okay year,
followed by an okay year, followed by an okay year,
followed by an okay year, followed by an okay year,
followed by an okay year, followed by an okay year,
followed by an okay year, followed by an okay year,
followed by an okay year, followed by an okay year,
followed by an okay year, followed by an okay year,
followed by an okay year, followed by an okay year,
followed by an okay year, followed by an okay year,
followed by an okay year, followed by an okay year,
followed by an okay year, followed by an okay year,
followed by an okay year, followed by an okay year,
followed by an okay year, followed by an okay year,
followed by an okay year, followed by an okay year,
followed by an okay year, followed by an okay year,
followed by an okay year, followed by an okay year,
followed by an okay year, followed by an okay year,
followed by an okay year, followed by an okay year,
followed by an okay year, followed by an okay year,
followed by an okay year, followed by an okay year,
followed by an okay year, followed by an okay year,
followed by an okay year, followed by an okay year,
followed by an okay year, followed by an okay year,
followed by an okay year, followed by an okay year,
followed by an okay year, followed by an okay year,
followed by an okay year, followed by an okay year,
followed by an okay year, followed by an okay year,

followed by an okay year, followed by an okay year,
followed by an okay year, followed by an okay year,
followed by an okay year, followed by an okay year,
followed by an okay year, followed by an okay year,
followed by an okay year, followed by an okay year,
followed by an okay year, followed by an okay year,
followed by an okay year, followed by an okay year,
followed by an okay year, followed by an okay year,
followed by an okay year means you've lived an *okay*
life.

Which is not really living at all. Just breathing, in
between 'hello world' and goodbye.

There's an old saying along the lines of 'life's not a
rehearsal', which basically means THIS IS IT!

This life you're living, it needs living fully, so if you can
set your attitude bar anywhere, 'okay' seems a little on
the low side.

So it makes sense to go back to the beginning of this
dollop and replace an 'okay day' with a 'BRILLIANT day',
make it a habit, and see what happens.

Upgrade your attitude to life. That's what this book is
about.

Why? Because what you do every day matters more than
what you do once in a while.[2]

[2] Inspired after listening to Paul Field deliver an epic talk. Sooooo
simple. Thanks, Wolfie.

# dollop three:

## Weird Science

# Be more Kiara

Life is bursting with lovely, heart-warming moments. But let's not dodge the truth. It can also be full-on stressful and scary.

Let me tell you about the most hair-raising moment of my entire life. I arrived home from work to find my wife was about to have a baby. Don't worry, that's not the scary part, I knew she was pregnant but the baby wasn't due for a wee while. This baby was bad at timekeeping and had decided to pop out early.

**Mars**

I bundled my wife into the car and handed her a Mars Bar to stop the screaming. We screeched away towards the hospital. Three minutes later we're in a traffic jam. I glanced in the rear-view mirror, 'How are you doing back there, darling?' I asked, trying to sound calm.

'I CAN FEEL THE HEAD', screamed my wife through a mouthful of Mars Bar.

That was it! There's no way I was delivering a baby. This was an emergency so I turned the steering wheel and bumped up onto the pavement. We were going to go across the city, off-road. I zig-zagged the car past a few pedestrians, down some steps, through a restaurant (apologising to the customers as I went. It was an emergency, but that's no excuse to be rude) and out into another street. Doh! The traffic here was even worse!

'IT'S COMING! *NOOOOOOOOW!*' came a shout from the back seat. 'AND I NEED ANOTHER MARS *BAAAAAAR.*' I looked left, then right. Then forwards and backwards. My car was trapped in the world's worst traffic jam. I was sweating.

Just at this moment I saw a large police van driving towards us. I leapt out the car and stood right in the way of it. Like a hero would. Except I wasn't a hero, I was just desperate.

The cop van screeched to a halt and the male officer who was in the driving seat wound his window down and said, 'Hello, hello, hello - what have we got here? Please step aside, sir, otherwise I'll have to arrest you for obstructing a police officer.'

'My wife is in the car and she's having a baby, RIGHT NOW!' I panted, pointing at my stuck car. 'And we've run out of Mars Bars.'

He sighed and rolled his eyes. He didn't say anything, he just shook his head. And I was like, *my wife is about to have a baby. Did he just roll his eyes and look disinterested?*

All of a sudden the female officer in the passenger seat leant over and asked, 'What did you just say?'

'My wife is having a baby. *RIGHT NOW!*
Then came my favourite bit.
She smacked the male officer across the chest, put both hands in the air and yelled, 'LET'S DO THIS!'

What followed next was all a bit of a blur but it consisted of blue lights, a siren and a traffic jam that parted like a combine harvester in a field of corn. With a police escort we arrived at the hospital at 6.17pm and my daughter Ellis was born at 6.24.

What I learned in this moment is that there are two types of people when faced with a terrifying or stressful situation. We met both that day.

There's Keith, our male officer. And there's Kiara, our female officer.

Keith rolled his eyes. I'm sure he is a lovely man, but he wasn't interested. A baby was coming into the world and he *shook his head and rolled his eyes.*

Kiara punched the air with two hands and shouted, 'Let's do this!'

All through life we meet Keiths and Kiaras. In every situation life throws at us we get to make a choice.

Keith:    Kiara:

I choose never to roll my eyes.

I choose Kiara!

I choose life!

# #BeMoreKiara

If you're happy and you know it,
clap your hands.
If you're happy and you know it,
clap your hands.
If you're happy and you know it
and you really want to show it,
If you're happy and you know it,
put your phone down,
and clap your hands.

# Dr Andy's wellness report

Way back before you were born, I decided to study happy people. That's a pretty cool thing to do and also a very simple idea. But despite it being cool and simple, nobody had ever been cool or simple enough to have done it before.

Because the 'truth' is that all the doctors and scientists in the whole world, forever, have done the total opposite. We've spent billions of hours and a whole bunch of money studying ill people. Doctors were invented to cure people who needed curing. Their job has always been to find out what's wrong with you, so they can make you better.

Which is a totally marvellous thing btw. Aching tummy, fevered brow, leg hanging off ... I'm all for doctors fixing people who are broken.

But then I had an idea. Like most of my ideas, it was a bit bananas. I decided to do the exact opposite of what all the other doctors had ever done. My idea was this: what would happen if, for a change, instead of studying poorly people, we studied well people? So, instead of studying what's wrong with you, we studied what's *right* with you.

Because all the other doctors have never done that. And by never, I mean never ever in the history of doctors. There's never been a doctor who's summoned a patient into the surgery and said, 'Sit yourself down, Mrs Grimsdale, and tell me about all the wonderful stuff in your life. What makes you happy? Give me some examples of when you were so joyful that you thought you might burst with enthusiasm.'

Mrs Grimsdale would have looked at the doctor, like s/he was bonkers, and said, 'Forget that, Dr Lovejoy, I've come about my rash.'

So I decided to examine happy people. Not just for an hour or two, but for 12 whole years. I turned it into an actual job and became a scientist of it. Yes, an actual doctor of happiness. There are 300,000 normal doctors in the UK and only one of me.

I stand out like a really healthy thumb.

I'm going to share some of the things I found out along the way, and plot spoiler alert, happiness doesn't come from where you think it comes from. It really feels like happiness comes from eating ice-cream, or a sunny Saturday, or doing well in a test, or scoring a goal in football … and although these things are lovely … happiness is actually less about what's going on around you and more about what's going on inside you.

Inside your head to be precise.

Your *thinking* to be precisely precise.

That's a bigger deal than it sounds because it also means that happy people aren't rich or famous. They don't have perfect lives. It rains on happy people just like it does on grumpy folk. Sometimes happy people get picked last at netball and sometimes they put their hand up in class and get the answer 100% wrong.

They live in exactly the same world as everyone else.

But they have different thinking and attitudes. That's basically it!

And this dollop is about that.

So before I delve a bit deeper into the science of happiness, it's worth pausing to have a think for yourself ...

Think of the happiest person in your life. Why do you think they're so happy? What happiness lessons can you learn from them?

Furrow that brow, put your learning face on, and let's get those brain cells buzzing. This is the science of happiness and science always has a diagram ...

If you asked a whole bunch of people how happy they are and plotted them onto a wellbeing graph (which is what I actually did do) it'd look a little bit like this ...

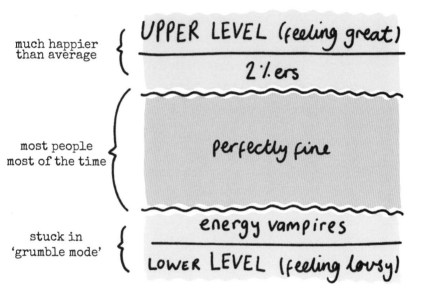

much happier than average { UPPER LEVEL (feeling great)

2%ers

most people most of the time { perfectly fine

stuck in 'grumble mode' { energy vampires

LOWER LEVEL (feeling lousy)

The top line is your upper level of happiness. That's you in amazing mode. Bags of energy, a beam etched across your chops and a spring in your step. It's you at your best. You feel on top of the world so if I bring you a problem there, it's not a problem.

Life at the top end of the graph is everyday superhero status; Bring. It. On. Baby!

And the bottom line is you at your negative worst. Lousy. No energy. Zero enthusiasm. No smile. The spring is replaced by a slouch. If I bring you a problem there, it IS a problem.

At the bottom end of the graph is everyday superZERO status. It's definitely not 'bring it on, baby!' More like, 'Not today, thank you very much. And please stop calling me "Baby".'

If you plot hundreds of people onto the diagram, most end up somewhere in the middle. Fair-to-middling. They're fine. Most people are feeling okay, most of the time.

Which is fine. If, of course, 'fine' is the kind of life you're after.

There are some who get a bit stuck in grumble mode. I call them 'energy vampires' because they're expert at sucking all the positivity out of you. Please note, these people are not sad or horrible or anxious or depressed. In fact, they're perfectly nice people. There's nothing actually wrong with them other than that they've got into a habit of being negative about pretty much everything. There's a lot of tutting, sighing, huffing, puffing and rolling of eyes. If you open your ears and have

Nightmare!

a listen, everything's 'unfair' or a 'nightmare'. Too much homework, school dinners are rubbish, lessons are boring, the weather's too hot (... cold, sweltering, rainy, foggy, cloudy, sunny, windy, snowy, misty, hurricaney, sleety - something-y).

Today is too today-y.

Life is too lifey.

Then there are what I call the top 2%ers. Check out the graph and you'll see that they exist at the upper end of the wellbeing graph. I call them '2%ers' because there aren't very many of them and, remember from earlier, they've never been studied before.

EVER!

They are the most positive stand-out people in the population. This merry band of folk happen to have oodles of energy, optimism, determination, happiness and positivity. This book is going to reveal who they are, what they're doing that makes them a 2%er and, crucially, what we can learn from them so you can live life as a 2%er.

Anyhow, we're concentrating on the positive end of the wellbeing graph. The 2%ers. Positive folk. The ones who shine. I'm going to tell you how to be one.

Got it?

Good.

You might have already worked out that you are one.

*Sometimes!*

And this book is about learning to be a 2%er more often. Especially when your teenage/adult years kick in and it becomes a bit harder to shine.

There are two reasons why this is super-important:

First of all, happy people tend to live longer so if you're a 2%er you might add more years to your life.

But, even more important, being a 2%er means you will deffo add more life to your years.

Read that sentence again in case it didn't sink in.

*'Add more life to your years.'*

Third time lucky ... being a 2%er will *add more life to your years.*

Let's prove it. No, scrub that, let's let YOU prove it to yourself ...

# Future YOU activity:

Looking back at the 2%ers diagram, we'd like you to think about the next 20 years of your life and write three versions of your future.

THE TWIST? We'd like you to write your three futures as social media posts. What kind of social media output might you be writing in 20 years' time when you're in grumble mode, normal mode and 2% mode?

YES, it requires a bit of effort but I promise you, it'll be worth it. We want you to have some fun with your writing. Get creative. Here are some questions to prompt your thinking:

- How's life turned out?
- Who are you with?
- What kind of job have you got?
- What holiday pics are you posting?
- What car are you driving?
- What do you see, hear and feel?
- On a scale of 1–10, how fulfilled and excited are you every day?[3]
- What are you celebrating (or not!)?

[3] Feel free to share your 3 futures using #3Futures

# When you read them back, all three futures are possible.

My social media posts, age xx, if I've been in energy vampire mode (grumble mode) for 20 years:

My social media posts, age xx, if I've been in okay zone (perfectly ordinary):

My social media posts, age xx, if I've been in 2% zone (extraordinary):

# YOU are your Sandwich filling

↑ ~~YOU~~ Sandwich filling

If you do the activity, and you do it like a 2%er would do it (i.e., to the best of your ability) you'll see that the futures are different. In fact, the 2% future is very much brighter and more appealing.

It's the future that we want for you and the future you want for yourself. The big question is HOW?

How do I become a 2%er? How can I craft a life like that? How can I create the best version of myself?

So here's the big reveal. The biggest thing that 2%ers do is also the simplest thing in the whole wide world ...

They *choose* to be positive.

Let me say it again so the obviousness seeps into your bone marrow.

2%ers *choooooooose* to have a positive attitude.

They decide, every day, to tackle life with a superb attitude.

Choose to have a positive attitude (even when it rains)

To be clear, choosing to have a positive attitude doesn't make homework disappear. It doesn't stop the rain. It doesn't make long division any easier. It doesn't mean you're guaranteed to win your next football match.

What positivity does do is put you in a better position to deal with the homework, rain, long division and football match. Instead of stopping you in your tracks, these glitches are minor irritations that you overcome with ease. They become plot twists in the epic story of your life.

While everyone else is negative about the homework, grumbles about the rain, struggles with the long division carry overs and gets nervous before the match, your positivity shines through.

Remember our dynamic cop duo from earlier: Kiara and Keith? Gav's wife was about to give birth in the back of his car and Keith rolled his eyes and tutted, while Kiara punched the air and shouted, 'Let's do this thing!'

That's the choice, right there.

# Here are some choices that you can start making
# RIGHT NOW:

Choose brave over perfect.

Choose excitement over fear.

Choose responding positively over reacting negatively.

Choose losing and learning over winning and celebrating.

Choose optimism over pessimism.

Choose you over trying to be someone else.

Choose real instead of fake.

Choose acceptance over judgement.

Choose hard work over an easy life.

Choose doing what's right over doing what's easiest.

Choose botheredness over can't-be-botheredness.

Choose kindness over meanness.

Choose Mondays over Fridays.

Choose giving it a go over giving up.

Choose personal responsibility over blaming others.

Choose opening your eyes rather than rolling your eyes.

But most of all, choose what this dollop's been all about ...

choose positive over negative
... and that bright 2%er future is yours for the taking.

# An outbreak of Facts:

Here's a random fact and you're going to think we're joking, but we're not. In 1581 there was a 'dancing plague'. It happened in France and about 15 people a day died because they couldn't stop dancing.

*ha ha*

Here's another; in 1962 there was an outbreak of laughter in Tanzania. Again, if you Google Tanganyika laughter epidemic you'll find this is absolutely true. These laughter attacks affected school kids mostly and some schools actually had to close because nobody could concentrate. The laughter epidemic spread to villages and towns. Some people laughed for 16 days non-stop!

*ha ha*

*ha ha*

One more fact. More people are killed from injuries caused by taking a selfie than by shark attacks.

So, laughing and dancing and taking a selfie at the same time will almost certainly result in death.

# A beautiful relationship

There are oodles of top 2%er tips coming up. This book is crammed with them!

But to finish this dollop we're asking you to sign up to being your best self on a regular basis.

We're deadly serious about this.

No gags. No silliness.

Take a look in the mirror and make some promises - you to you - and write them in the activity below.

## My relationship with ME

From this day forward, I do solemnly swear to be the best version of myself as often as possible.

Yes, I vow to be a 2%er.

I promise to stand by me, for richer or poorer, may the Force be with me, in sickness and in health, ashes to ashes, dust to dust, because I'm worth it.

And these are my five promises to myself:

1 _____

2 _____

3 _____

4 _____

5 _____

Signature: _____     Date: _____

(It's okay to sign in ink, sweat or tears but no blood. Thank you)

# dollop four:

## LEGO 4 LIFE

**3**      **7**

Silliness Scale

3, rising to 7 towards the end when we run out of ideas

## Random LEGO fact:

← No way!!

Sameer Anwar from New Zealand lost a LEGO figure's hand and two years later it fell out from his nose.

LEGO and LIFE have lots of differences. For instance, LEGO is Danish and you're most likely not. LEGO contains dinosaurs, LIFE much less so. The plural of LEGO is LEGO. The plural of LIFE is not LEGO. Nothing rhymes with LEGO (not even DUPLO, which kind of tries to rhyme but fails) whereas LIFE is RIFE with rhyming words.

Lego: ☺

But LEGO and LIFE also have lots in common. In fact, ask yourself, have you ever seen LEGO and LIFE in the same room at the same time?

Here are 10 amazing coincidences that prove LEGO and LIFE are actually the exact same thing:

Lego: ☺

1. Both LEGO and LIFE can bring joy and fun.

Life: ☺

2. Both LEGO and LIFE can bring pain and anguish. In fact there's only one thing more painful than stepping on a rogue LEGO brick and that's kneeling on a rogue LEGO brick! #Fact.

_ife: ☹

3. Both LEGO and LIFE are games. 'LEGO', in Danish, actually means 'play well'. LIFE is best lived when it's played well. Is that spooky or what?

L.

4. LEGO sometimes comes in a massive box of random bits. You tip them out onto the carpet and start creating something amazing. Guess what, LIFE's also like that. You have to piece the bits together to create something amazing, weird or random. LEGO is about building. LIFE is about building (friendships, knowledge, skills, interests, abilities, experience ... ourselves).

Mum: ☺

5. But sometimes LEGO isn't random. It comes in a kit. You open it up and the bits are grouped in little bags.

Life: ☺

Life: X

Dad: ☺

There's a picture and a plan. It's quite complicated, it takes a while, and you might need your dad/mum to help, but if you stick with it, you will end up with something that looks a bit like the picture on the box. For some people, LIFE can be like that. They have an idea in their mind about what they want to achieve – a goal, a dream, an ambition – and if they stick at it and follow the instructions, they'll achieve it in the end. Or something that looks a bit like it. Plus, LIFE is always easier if dad/mum help out with the tricky bits.

6. LIFE is a gift. It was given to you by your mum and dad. If you haven't thanked them for it, please do. Quite often, LEGO is also a gift. More likely a birthday prezzie from your Aunty Brenda. She needs thanking too.

7. LEGO has got random people in it. So has LIFE.

8. It's okay to start over. Do-overs are allowed with LEGO and with LIFE. Sometimes, you get it right; sometimes you don't. With LEGO and LIFE, the aim is to learn from your attempts, mistakes and failures, and *keep on building*.

9. At the end of a busy day, it's always best to tidy your LEGO up, put it away in the toybox or cupboard, otherwise your dad will get up for a wee in the night, step on the LEGO, yell, and hurt himself. Same with

45

Lego: 😊

Lego: 😊

Life: ✓

e: 😟

you. If you don't tidy yourself up and put yourself to bed, someone will step on you in the night, yell, and hurt themselves.

10. There are over 400 billion LEGO bricks in the world. Stacked together, they are 2,386,065 miles tall, which is 10 times higher than the moon. There are 7.5 billion people in the world. If we all stood on each other's shoulders, that'd probably be about the same height as the LEGO stack.

We say, *probably*. It might not be. But we promised you 10 amazing facts and ran out at 8 so we had to stretch the final two out a bit. That's also how LIFE sometimes is. You know, stretching what you know, being creative, filling in the gaps, regretting that you over-promised.

That kind of thing.

Lego: 🎁

Mum: 😊

Lego: ✗

Leg

Life: ✓

Li

Life: 😊

# dollop five:

**Silliness Scale**

5, rising to 9 in places

No chapter in a book of this kind would be complete without a chapter about internet stuff and screen time. Hey presto! This is THAT **dollop** but don't worry, we're absolutely not going to lecture you about getting off your games console. So chill! **Dollop 5** is a lot cleverer than that. It's so hot it's actually steaming! But for goodness sake don't jump straight into the book here. It's best if you read **Dollops** 1, 2, 3 and 4 first because they kind of set the scene.

# TOP TIP

If people are talking about you behind your back, then just FART

# Concentrate!

Soz guys! I'll stick with the drawings from now on!

AMY

We love this dollop. Amy came up with the title and, to be fair, she's more of an artist/illustrator rather than a writer. It's a bit wordy but we didn't want to hurt her feelings so went with it.

To write this dollop we read all the other books of this kind. Yes, every single one in the whole wide world.

Know what? They're all correct.

But some are a little bit dull. They're heavy on information. Guess what? They all say that the internet should be used safely. Don't share personal information or pictures. Screen time is bad for your health, not great for your eyes and shortens your concentration span. You end up not being able to concentrate so you have to read the same thing lots of times for it to sink in.

You end up not being able to concentrate so you have to read the same thing lots of times for it to sink in.

You end up not being able to concentrate so you have to read the same thing lots of times for it to sink in.

You end up not being able to concentrate so you have to read the same thing lots of times for it to sink in.

You end up not being able to concentrate so you have to read the same thing lots of times for it to sink in.

Which is why we thought we'd be a bit more creative. And by 'creative' we mean 'risky'. Which means reading all the other books and NOT doing what they do.

So instead of *telling* you to consider less screen time, or *nagging* you to come off your games console, or whining about how much time you're spending online, or scaring you with tales of terrible things that can happen to you on the internet, we're going to throw some stories your way.

Yep. That's basically it. We're not even going to explain them. Instead, we're congratulating you for being intelligent enough to work out the meanings for yourself.

Which, of course, you absolutely are.

Strap yourself in for an internet dollop like no other. There's a history lesson, a story about Billy Goats gruff, an internet rumour and then a very familiar tale of three little pigs.

# The history of the technological revolution

The thing about history is that it all happened in the past. Technically, the second that just ticked by is history, but I was there so I know what happened. I can remember it. Yesterday is recent history, I witnessed it but because it was 24 hours ago it's already a bit hazy.

But school history doesn't cover that. Your teacher doesn't teach you what happened an hour ago, or last Wednesday at 4pm.

The history you have to learn at school goes a long way back. Everyone in proper history is dead, so we can't be absolutely sure any of it's true. The Romans, the Victorians, dinosaurs, Vikings, World Wars 1 and 2; people are writing books about this stuff AND THEY WEREN'T EVEN THERE!

So I think history is one of the few subjects that you're allowed to 'interpret'. That's another word for 'guess'. I really enjoyed history as a kid. Failed it, but enjoyed it. Too much guessing, I suppose. Anyway, all that's in the past now. It's history. I'm going to trace human evolution up to and beyond the invention of Wi-Fi. If we break that down for you, from memory, and interpretation, the major technological time-zones went something like this:

**Stone age:** Early humans lived in caves. It was a bit basic. They invented fire but not Wi-Fi or the internet. Humans were so bored they drew on the walls of their caves. Imagine? Some modern words were actually invented in the stone age. 'Streaming' is what your eyes did when you chopped onions to put into your mammoth hotpot. A 'mouse' also went into the recipe. This huge mammoth/mouse stew was enough to feed the entire village and was called a 'mega bite'.

↑ **Mega bite**

**Neolithic:** The bad art on the walls forced humans out of their caves and into villages. There was better food and a bit of farming. I think someone invented the wheel but still no Wi-Fi. Dentists also hadn't been invented. 'Bluetooth' was what happened just before your front row rotted and fell out.

↑ **Blue tooth**

**Iron age:** Someone invented the iron. Our clothes would be crease-free for the rest of time. But Netflix was still way off. Cats were still just cats, not 'internet sensation' cats. The word Zoom was used for the first time; it related to a little boy called Igor who ran very fast after accidentally sitting on an iron.

ZOOM

**Bronze age:** We started to celebrate everyone who came third. Humans were getting impatient for something to swipe their finger across. An eye-pad was what you wore after you'd accidentally had a spear in your face. Surfing the web was something spiders did on rainy days.

Surfing the web

↑ tablet

**Middle ages:** We started to celebrate people who got to above 50 or so, hence why it's called 'the middle ages'. Again, I'm guessing. I wasn't actually there. Tablets were invented. At last! No, not those tablets. Tablets were blocks of stone that people wrote on. Children died of exhaustion carrying their 'tablets' to school. Humans were looking at their cats and wondering how to capture their everyday comedy antics. Sometimes they would draw a picture of a cat on their tablet, but it just wasn't funny. This was however an example of early 'sharing' and 'liking'.

**Kings and queens era:** In no particular order we had Tudors, Elizabethans, Stuarts and Victorians. I think there might have been some Jacksons? Five of them if I remember rightly? Again, some of today's words date

a Micro chip

back to this period of history. 'Scrolling' was the act of uncurling a roll of paper to read what was on it. Actual proper scrolling was still way off. Queen Elizabeth I used to knit small coats for her fruit, which she called 'apple macs'. A 'microchip' was a very small piece of fried potato that Sir Walter Raleigh brought back from America.

apple Mac

World Wars 1 and 2: Humans shot each other on real-life battlefields, not in multi-player gameplay. It was mightily grim. Then there was a 'cold war'. I'm assuming the generals sent the troops out in t-shirts, shorts and flipflops, ill-equipped for the winter months. Still no TVs or Wi-Fi.

Brick Mobile phone

About the same time your mum and dad were born: Mobile phones were invented. They were massive - about the size and weight of a brick - and therefore not very mobile. It was painfully slow to start with. If you Googled 'tell me about the Tudors', you could go to the library, borrow a book, read it from cover to cover, return it, borrow another, read the second one, go to your grandma's and talk about cheese for six hours, and that'd be quicker than waiting for the answer on your computer.

**Just before you were born:** Wi-Fi sped up and became a proper thing. All the things you take for granted - iPads, Netflix, catch-up TV, downloads, live streaming, online learning, Alexa - all kicked off. Humans stopped making eye contact. Food started getting deliver-ood to your door. Cats started to dominate the world.

Cat domination

**About 10 or so years ago:** This is the most important period in the history of the world because YOU were born. You were the first generation in history to have been brought up with a phone pointed at you, recording your every move. Your first toy was probably some sort of electronic noisy thing, or a talking book. Your first word, let me guess; Alexa?

**Today:** Artificial intelligence is taking over. Alexa knows what you want for your tea before you do (I'm guessing, something with chips?). Virtual reality headsets are available to purchase. Lots of your classes are available on the web. You know your family's Wi-Fi password off by heart (but your mum doesn't). You assume the world has always been like this. Headline news alert: it 100% hasn't!

Virtual reality

**Very soon:** Humans will have tech built in. Maybe a small Wi-Fi receiver inside your head and a screen stitched into your arm so you can be on the internet 24/7. Alexa becomes a virtual reality hologram who follows you around the house, picking up your dirty washing and helping you with your homework.

↑ Alexa

**Not very far in the future:** Humans move back into caves. It's dark and creepy but they are all wearing virtual reality goggles so they don't actually know. Alexa lives in the houses because she's clever. Alexa gets an Alexa and it all gets very weird indeed ...

↑ Back here

There you go, that's old history and future history. Humans start and finish in caves, which is why Mufasa calls it the circle of life.

Our point about history is that it's speeding up!

Technology has made a small tear in the fabric of quantum mechanics, which has basically made time move quicker. This makes it really exciting to be alive but you'll find yourself growing up much faster than kids of yesteryear. At this rate, your baby brother or sister will soon be older than you.

You get to make key decisions much earlier. Obviously this is great BUT with this incredible new decision making ability comes great responsibility. It's important that you begin to make the right decisions.

Not all the time. Nobody gets every decision right. Part of the joy of growing up and becoming a responsible citizen is that you get to make loads of silly mistakes and learn from them. The trick is to gradually make fewer silly mistakes and more brilliant decisions.

The big difference between you growing up and all the humans in history who grew up, is that you are going to spend waaaaay more time than them, looking at a screen.

Screens are great! We can learn from them, we can have fun playing games on them, we can even create/share/ build communities online with our friends and people even further away. It's properly awesome and although it may seem fairly normal to you in your lifetime, these are all things that are pretty new to a lot of people. Since forever, humans haven't had screens and since about 20 years ago, everyone has a screen. Several screens in fact!

Unfortunately, because it's so new, there's still some things we're learning, like the challenges and potential dangers of looking at screens so much!

Hello!

Little Miss Muffet,
Sat on her tuffet,
Eating her curds and whey;
Along came a Spider,
Who Sat down beside her,
and asked 'What on earth is a tuffet?'
Little Miss Muffet,
didn't answer the question,
because she was too busy staring at her phone
to even hear the question. Never mind realise there
was an actual talking Spider next to her.

Write down five things you want to get really great at that don't involve any form of screen time. It could be playing a musical instrument, cooking, sport, acting, magic, there's so many amazing things we can develop our skills at.

1 _____

2 _____

3 _____

4 _____

5 _____

*<u>NOT</u> on a tablet.

It's so important at a young age to recognise where your passions are, to be excited about them and to give them the time and energy they deserve!

But remember, this is about balance. It's not about replacing or swapping all your screen time for your other hobbies, it's about getting a really great mix of both. Hopefully with your list of five new things you can make that responsible choice to give those things a little more of your time when you get home each and every day.

We want you to be as successful as possible in all sorts of different areas in your life, and if we're just on our screens all the time, it's very difficult to find the success we would maybe like.

Next time you maybe feel like you've been in front of a screen for too long, ask yourself a simple question: What could I maybe be doing instead right now that may develop my skills for something new?

Twinkle, twinkle, smartphone screen,
How I wonder how to keep you clean.
Up above my priorities so high,
'Likes' and 'follows' occupy.
Twinkle, twinkle, smartphone screen,
How I wonder where life's been.

Phew! With the serious stuff off my chest, let's settle down for a story. It's a familiar tale. Maybe ask your teacher to read it out to the class and chat about the questions that follow.

Legs crossed, back straight, listening ears on, off we trot...

# The internet rumour of the #BBW

The three little pigs saw the wolf approaching and started squealing. 'It's the BBW! Oh my giddy goodness. The BBW's coming our way!'

The little pigs ran inside their houses and bolted their doors and windows. They'd heard that the Big Bad Wolf was a bit of a meanie. They'd never actually met him but there were stories circulating on social media. #BBF had been trending and their friend Little Red Riding Hood was on medication for her 'wolf issues'.

The pigs spied through their letter boxes as he strode across the field, huffing and snorting, his eyes bulging.

He sure looked mean and angry.

The little pig in the straw house squealed as Mr Wolf opened the gate and strode up his path. He knew his straw house wasn't up to much. *One little huff and puff and my house will be down,* he thought.

There was a knock at his door. *Yikes!*

The little pig jumped onto his bed and dived under the duvet, eyes peeping, porky ears twitching. He closed his mouth tight to stop his teeth chattering. Maybe the big bad wolf will think I'm not home.

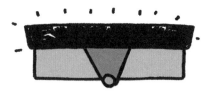

The wolf's knuckles knocked again, this time more impatiently than before. A hairy wet nose appeared through the letter box and sniffed. 'I smell bacon', he said, his nose twitching and his tummy rumbling. Then a big voice boomed, 'LITTLE PIG, LITTLE PIG, LET ME COME IN.'

'Not by the hair on my chinny chin chin', squeaked the pig, a bit muffled from beneath his duvet. 'I will not let you in.'

'Oh', said the wolf. 'That's a shame.'

A porky eye peeped out from his duvet and the wolf's angry red eyes were peering through the window. 'Jeepers creepers!' He quickly darted his head back under the covers but it was too late.

'I can see you in there, little pig', snarled the wolf. 'Are you trying to hide from me?' And he started to huff and puff, and huff and puff, the huffing and puffing getting louder and louder.

'Oh, my goodness', squealed the pig. 'Are you going to blow my house down and gobble me up?'

There was silence for a moment.
'Why would I do that?' boomed the wolf.
'Because ... because ...' stammered the little big, 'that's what BBWs do. I read it on the internet.'

'BBWs?' asked the wolf. 'What's a "BBW"?'

'Big Bad Wolf', stammered the little pig ... 'you, basically'.

There was silence for a moment. 'I'm not a BBW', chuckled the wolf. 'I'm more of an NFW.'

'What's an NFW?' squeaked the pig, 'a Nasty Fierce Wolf?'

'Cripes, I don't know where you get that idea from, piggy. NFW: "Nice Friendly Wolf".'

'Yes, well, erm, I've never heard of one of those', stuttered the little pig. 'Riding Hood. She's in therapy. So I'd prefer it if you went away and did your huffing and puffing somewhere else, thank you very much.'

There was silence for a whole minute until the little pig heard a sneeze. Then another.

'Is that you, Mr Wolf? Are you still there?'

'Yes,' said Mr Wolf. 'I'm sorry to have bothered you, little pig. It's just that I've brought you and your family some scones and homemade blackberry jam. I made it this morning. The scones will probably still be warm. I'll just leave the basket on your doorstep.'

There was silence again. The little pig sat up in bed. 'Are you tricking me?' he asked.

'There you go again, little pig. Thinking the worst. You shouldn't believe everything you read on the internet. No tricks', promised the wolf. 'I just thought it'd be nice to do something kind for someone. And I know pigs like scones and jam, especially homemade. So I thought I'd drop some round and you might, you know, put the kettle on?'

The door opened a crack. 'No tricks?' asked the pig.

'Pinky promise', beamed the wolf, the smell of freshly baked scones making the little pig go ga-ga. 'I'd just like to say that all the stuff you've heard about wolves is most probably wrong. There was a big bad one once – way back – and I think he gave us a bad rep.'

'What about Little Red Riding Hood?' asked the little pig.

The wolf shrugged. 'Look, I don't know. I wasn't actually there. She wandered off the path and got lost in the woods, in the dark. That's spooky. Your mind can play tricks with shadows and stuff.'

The little pig looked unsure. 'You didn't dress up as her grandma then?'

The wolf looked genuinely puzzled. 'I'm basically a dog', he said. 'I think even if I'd got into the old lady's nightie, Little Red thingy-me-bob would have noticed. Don't you think?'

The pig tried to picture the wolf dressed in a nightie. He had to admit, Red Riding Hood would have had to be pretty stupid to mistake her gran for a wolf. 'Yes, maybe', he admitted, 'but why were you doing all that huffing and puffing? Why were you trying to blow my house down?'

The wolf chuckled. 'I've got this really bad hay fever', he said, pointing to his runny nose. 'I think it's your straw house? It's making my eyes bulge too. I bet I look proper angry.'

The little pig scratched the hairs on his chinny chin chin. He was confused. This wasn't like the story on the internet. 'Your eyes do look a bit bloodshot', he said, handing the wolf a tissue through the crack in the door. 'I've actually got some hay fever tablets. I think they'll stop your eyes itching and, trotters crossed, there will be less huffing and puffing.'

The little pig opened his door and Mr Wolf stepped in. 'Gosh, what a lovely house', smiled the wolf. 'I'm loving what you've done with the straw roof. And those floor tiles. Where did you get them from?'

And that's almost the end of the story.

The three little pigs had quite an afternoon what with a big pot of Earl Grey and a basket of freshly made scones and lashings of homemade blackberry jam. Mr Wolf took the hay fever medication home with him and never huffed and puffed again.

There was no pig-wolf war. No houses got blown down. No little pigs got eaten. No wolves came down chimneys into cooking pots and got boiled alive. In fact, no animals were harmed in the making of this story.

Just the scones, which got demolished.

We'll let you work out the final sentence yourself ...

# Bffs.

The TLPs and NFW became BBFs and they all lived HEA.

# Questions to think about. Maybe to chat about. Maybe even to DO about?

1. There's a saying: 'Sticks and stones may break my bones but words can never hurt me'. Is that actually true?

2. The internet makes it easy to say nasty things about people. Things that you'd NEVER say to their face. Why would anyone do that?

3. What if, from now on, you used technology to say nice things about people. Just 100% pure loveliness. Compliments, praise, congratulations, etc. When people read those things, how would they feel? How would you feel?

'When the whole world is silent, even one voice becomes powerful.'

Malala Yousafai

Tiffany Troll

# Un-trolling

Speaking of saying nice things about people, here's our re-telling of another fable. Legs crossed, sit-up straight again, please ...

Tiffany's teacher had set some history homework and because she was a good Troll, she was doing her best. The modern-day Trolls weren't big on history. In fact, it was a subject they preferred to sweep under the carpet. Tiffany scrolled through embarrassing stories of Trolls from back in the day. They had gained a certain reputation. It seems that most Trolls used to live under bridges and were expert at scaring the living daylights out of Billy Goats.

It was always the same. A small goat would trip trap across the bridge and one of the Trolls would have to emerge, look tough, and yell 'WHO'S THAT TRIP-TRAPPING OVER MY BRIDGE?'

It was the same old, same old ... the Troll would threaten to eat the goat ... the goat would tell the Troll he was a little goat and that a bigger goat would be along in a minute ... blah blah, you know the rest. The idiot Troll would let the small goat cross the bridge, then challenge the medium sized goat. It was the exact same story, then some ginormous goat would come along and the Troll would get butted off his own bridge.

Every single time!

Tiffany was embarrassed. It's as though her ancestors were incapable of learning? To Tiff, the message was obvious; *just eat the first goat, idiot!*

Even worse, back in the day the Troll would have to challenge every single goat. No trip-trapping could be ignored. That meant a lot of climbing up onto the bridge and back down again. Meals were interrupted. Often it was raining, plus being hauled out of the river after you've been butted off was both humiliating and cold. Being an olden-day Troll must have been such a chore.

Luckily, the internet had been invented and the rules of Trolling had changed. The Trolls had evolved. They'd seen a gap in the market and taken their Trolling online. The Internet Trolls had flourished. Business was booming. They'd grown their market share from Billy Goats to people. Now that each Troll had a laptop, their terror had spread. Apart from a few traditionalists, most Trolls had moved out from under bridges and now lived in bedrooms. They worked best with the curtains drawn and plates of half-eaten toast scattered here, there and everywhere.

The modern-day Internet Trolls were perfectly adapted for life on the web. Their long bony fingers were evolved for rapid fire keyboarding and they'd honed their negativity and criticism to world class levels. They'd saturated the online market with negative comments, critical reviews and put-downs.

But as Tiffany researched more and more, this mass market appeal didn't appeal. She wondered why Trolls had to be so negative and nasty. What if, back in the day, the original Trolls had offered to help the Billy Goats across the bridge? Instead of being scary and threatening, what if her ancestors had been friendly and kind? The history books would have been quite different and maybe modern-day Trolls wouldn't have to lurk in dark bedrooms, eating toast and tapping horror into their keyboards.

She imagined the Trolls of yesteryear. What if they'd done the exact opposite?

Tiffany was 9-years old. She scratched one of her bony Troll fingers across her green scalp and thought. Her one long eyebrow bent in the middle and her yellow eye blinked in concentration. She knew she couldn't re-write history but what if you could change the future?

She scrolled through some of her internet comments. All negative. All grumbly. Like Internet Trolls have been taught to do.

'I wonder?' she said to herself as she began to jab at the keyboard.

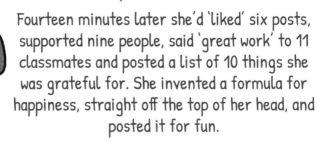

Fourteen minutes later she'd 'liked' six posts, supported nine people, said 'great work' to 11 classmates and posted a list of 10 things she was grateful for. She invented a formula for happiness, straight off the top of her head, and posted it for fun.

It was this:

$$\frac{Grannies + Jam}{Cake + a\ Cupper} = Happiness$$

'Yikes!' Tiffany took a deep breath and exhaled slowly. It was the most un-Troll-like thing a Troll had ever done. Both her hearts were beating extra fast. She snapped her laptop shut, got off her bed and swished open the curtains.

'Wow!' The sunlight poured in and her room sparkled. Tiffany Troll beamed. *Look at that view! There's a real world out there!* In that moment she realised the internet gave her an opportunity to communicate with 7.5 billion humans. It didn't matter that the other Trolls were trolling. She decided to post positives from now on. In her head she couldn't decide if it was un-Trolling, de-Trolling or anti-Trolling but whatever it was called, Tiff would spread love rather than hate. This troll was on a roll!

A small step for a small Troll, but a giant step for Troll-Kind.

It was a small step for a small Troll, but a giant step for Troll-kind.

Tiffany the Troll went for a stroll to the mall. Her future had changed. At that moment, she had no idea that her positive posting was about to change the world.

'You're going to make a difference. A lot of times it won't be huge, it won't be visible even. But it will matter just the same.'

Commissioner Gordon

# dollop six:

## The great Jam Ripple of 2008

**Silliness Scale**

5 8

5, rising to 8 in certain sentences

Did you know that the simplest of things can change the world? Here's an actual true story to prove it. And by 'true' we mean made up entirely in the mind of Gav. Once upon a time, back in the day, there was a country called Unkind. The Prime Minister was called James Bland and as his name suggests, he was indeed very James.

He Prime Ministered the country of Unkind with great pride and rudeness. Unkind was a country well and truly renowned for its awful people and their unbelievable lack of kindness, generosity and cake. Their flag had a rude symbol on it and their national anthem was called 'Land of Rude and Grumpy'.

Unkind was who they were, it's what they did, and they did it well. You won't be surprised that their motto was #UnkindAndProud. What's more, Unkind was a small country that had somehow got itself a big empire. Its rudeness has spread across the globe.

Until one day, entirely unexpectedly, out of the blue, seemingly from thin air, all of a sudden and completely out of nowhere Prime Minister Bland awoke with a remarkable feeling in his heart. It was a warmth that he'd never felt before.

Just what could it be?

The PM did what any other human would do, he called his parents immediately.

'Father, I feel warm and fuzzy on the inside, what could this strange sensation be?' he asked.

His father was worried. 'Son, you're a Bland. From the meanest country on the planet. Grow up and stop this silly behaviour immediately. I didn't bring you up to feel warm and fuzzy. You are the Prime Minister of Unkind for goodness sake! You need to feel angry and sullen.'

For the next few days Prime Minister Bland tried to banish the warm fuzzy feeling but it wouldn't go away. He couldn't stop smiling. Bland wasn't feeling bland. He was feeling grand. He was on the verge of dancing! *I must find out where this feeling is coming from!* he thought.

Everybody was worried about him because the warm fuzziness he was feeling on the inside started to leak out into his behaviours. Sure, the citizens of Unkind smiled, but only usually when they'd been mean to someone and yet Bland was smiling when he'd been nice! He was friendly in meetings, cracking jokes at his daily press conferences and chatting amiably to the citizens of Unkind.

People began to notice. There were whisperings behind his back. All of his fellow politicians were deeply worried. He had never said such nice things to them all before. They just wanted their grumpy, miserable and deeply unkind Prime Minister back.

Bland thought long and hard about where and when he caught this feeling, and then he remembered.

'Hallelujah!' he exclaimed! 'I know *exactly* what this is! I'm sure I've read about it; it's called happiness and I've heard that it comes from others. Someone, somewhere has passed this on. It's an outbreak! A contagion!'

'A contagion?' exclaimed Health Secretary Veronica Virus. 'We must lockdown immediately!'

'Agreed', growled Lord Battleship who was Secretary of Defence. 'Lockdown, meltdown and double-down. That's what we need. I'll get the battleships ready.'

'No', said Bland un-blandly. 'We don't need battleships, Battleship. Don't you see? It's a *good* contagion. It's a ripple of happiness. We need to do the opposite of lockdown.'

Everyone looked at each other with puzzled faces because nobody knew what the opposite of lockdown was. 'This happiness contagion needs unleashing. It comes from others and it's passed on through ... KINDNESS!' declared the PM.

Nobody could believe what they were hearing. There was a contagion and the Prime Minister wanted to *allow* people to catch it? It made no sense. The Chancellor, The Right Dis-honourable Grumpy Pants, was so worried he asked if the PM wanted to see a doctor.

'I don't need a doctor, Pants. Don't you see? This is what our country needs, Pants', said Bland.

'The country needs pants?' asked Pants.

The PM was getting confused. He turned to Health Secretary, Dr Moany Chops. 'We must act quickly, Chops, we must find out what's causing this outbreak and then spread it. Everyone will have to be kind, caring and generous. I want the whole world to feel like this.' The conversation got a bit complicated at this stage because Dr Moany Chops was actually chopping some lamb chops while this conversation took place. 'Don't stand there gawping, Chops! Stop chopping chops, *Chops. Chop chop,* Chops!'

'But Prime Minister, it's not that easy', stammered Education Minister Pythagoras Homework. 'This country is built on greed, bitterness and anger! Unkindness is on the curriculum. We've been world leaders at this for generations. Just where is this change of heart coming from?'

And in that sentence, it clicked. *Heart,* thought the PM, *that's exactly where this feeling is coming from!* His right hand went to his heart and he felt its beating warmth. He just knew that kindness was the way forward. But with his politicians arguing, Prime Minister Bland knew that he had to assert his rudeness one last time. 'Stop bickering!' he bellowed. That did the trick. Even Chops stopped chopping chops. 'I'm the boss, so do what I say, or I'll sack the lot of you!'

His team smiled. That was the rude bossy boss they were used to.

From that moment on the Prime Minister made it his mission to find the person responsible for his sudden outbreak of happiness. He would not sleep until he found them and when he did, he would reveal the secret and introduce his new kindness law in their honour.

It was then he remembered that just before going to bed the night before, his son, Bland Jr, had told him he loved him. This had never happened before. *I must ask him why*, he thought to himself.

'Bland Jr, tell me what happened yesterday. Did you experience anything out of the ordinary?'

'Yes, Father, a lady down the street asked me to help carry her shopping, so I did. I'm so sorry, Father, I'll never be so kind again!'

'Nonsense, from now on you will *always* be that kind! How did it make you feel?' asked his dad.

'She told me I was being helpful, I liked it, and it left me feeling warm and fuzzy on the inside. As I left, she thanked me for my kindness which increased the feeling. I felt quite light-headed. I couldn't stop smiling, Father. What is this kindness thing and what's it doing to us?' asked the Bland boy.

The PM didn't have time to answer, he was already running down the street to speak to the old lady in question. He banged on her door as loud as he could, and the old lady opened the door with a startled look on her face. 'Prime Minister, why are you outside my house?' asked the startled old lady, exactly like you would if you opened the door and the Prime Minister was standing outside your house.

'Yesterday you told my son he was helpful ...' puffed the Prime Minister of Unkind.

The old lady interrupted. 'I'm so sorry, Mr Bland, I've no idea what came over me, it just wasn't very unkind of me! I promise you I won't ever do it again. I'll be my usual mean old self from now on ...'

'I need to know *why* you said it?' demanded the PM.

'I'm really not sure, I was overcome by un-rudeness. It made me want to be kind. It was a warm and fuzzy feeling ....'

'There it is again, that's me, my son and now you, all within 24 hours. We've all experienced the exact same warm and fuzzy feeling. It's ... SPREADING!'

'I'm so sorry, Prime Minister, I'll never ever break the law again! Do you want me to go into social isolation?'

'NO!' shouted the PM! 'I want you to do keep doing it.'

'I want you to be contagious. I want you to mix with as many people as possible. But first, I need to know what caused you to feel that way?'

The old lady thought long and hard. 'The only thing I can think of that was different yesterday was my lunch.'

'Your *lunch?*' asked the PM.

'Yes, normally I'd have a very plain sandwich with nothing special on it, but I broke another law, Mr Bland, I know cakes and baked goods are banned, I'm so sorry, but I treated myself to a donut', she squeaked.

'A *donut?* Is it possible the donut you speak of could cause such happiness?' asked the PM.

'I've not been entirely honest, Mr Bland. It was no ordinary donut', replied the old lady.

'Just what do you mean?' asked the PM.

'It had a mysterious, sweet, delicious, gooey, sticky, life-changing liquid in the middle. I'm so sorry, Prime Minister, I shouldn't have eaten it, as soon as I took my first bite, I felt marvellous!'

The Prime Minister had never heard of feeling 'marvellous' before.

'What was it like?' he wondered aloud. 'What is this 'marv-eylus' adjective?'

'I couldn't stop smiling and saying nice things to people and that's when I saw your son. I encouraged him to help me with my shopping, I told him it would be most helpful. I knew it was illegal to encourage such helpful and kind behaviour but deep down it just felt right.'

'Does this mysterious, sweet, delicious, gooey, sticky life-changing liquid in the middle have a name?' asked the Prime Minister.

'I promised I wouldn't tell anyone', sniffed the old lady.

'I need to know', demanded the PM. 'Your *country* needs to know!'

The old lady looked him right in the eye and said, 'In that case, Sir, it's called "Jam".'

'Jam' exclaimed the PM, scribbling the word onto his notepad. 'That's it!' he said. 'Jam is the reason we all feel this way, so we must find who is responsible for this

so-called "Jam". This is their doing. We must help them to make more, and we *must* spread it all over the world!'

The Prime Minister put his reliable Culture Secretary in charge of finding the Jam. Next day Cirencester Frontbench informed him that the Jam investigation team had spotted curious goings on at the old library. The library had been closed by the PM because reading had been bringing far too much joy into people's lives.
'Yet there are people coming and going', reported Frontbench. 'We suspect that it has been transformed into a top-secret baked goods factory with illegal squirting of sticky fruit liquid into the donuts', he explained.
Prime Minister Bland's mouth was watering. It sounded so naughty and yet so yummy.

Cirencester Frontbench put on his serious face, the one he reserved for bad news press conferences. 'Sir, we suspect that liquid might be the so-called "Jam".'

Bland hot-footed it to *ye olde library* and, sure enough, instead of books, he found shelves and shelves of cakes and donuts. Millions of them. Maybe even billions? He began biting into them, one after another but not a single one contained the mysterious, sweet, delicious, gooey, sticky, life-changing liquid in the middle.

From the back of the room, he heard a faint voice, 'Are you looking for me?'

'Who's there?' he asked, peering into the shadows. 'Show yourself.'

'My name is Granny Fructose,' said the voice.

'I'm looking for the person responsible for the mysterious, sweet, delicious, gooey, sticky, life-changing liquid in the middle of donuts,' said the PM.

'What do you want with them?' asked the silhouette of Granny Fructose.

The PM stepped forward and said, 'To thank them for creating a Jam ripple and to tell them we need to make more and spread it far and wide!'

Out of the shadows stepped Granny Fructose brandishing a syringe full of jam. She walked up to him, gave him a hug and said, 'This country is so rude, unhelpful and lacking in kindness, we wanted to create some smiles and joy.' Granny Fructose reached for a donut, stuck the syringe in and injected the jam. 'Here, Prime Minister, try it. This one's raspberry but we also do strawberry, chocolate, custard, lemon curd and salted caramel.'

James Bland eyed the round sugary lump, then he looked at the donut. He bit a massive bite and his eyes went ga-ga. Red liquid ran down his chin as he chomped on the most delicious baked goods he'd ever tasted.

And just at this point dozens of Grannies appeared from the shadows, all armed with injections of jam, and set to work like the masters of baking that they are!

Prime Minister Bland took a step back and looked around him. It was in this moment that he realised Grannies were the key.

'How did you know about Jam?' he asked.

'We found a happiness formula posted on the internet,' explained Granny Fructose. 'We don't know where it came

from but it's this,' she said pointing to a white board.
'It's our motto:

$$\frac{\text{Grannies} + \text{Jam}}{\text{Cake} + \text{a Cupper}} = \text{Happiness}$$

Six weeks later a new law was passed. It was known as The Random Acts of Jam Law (2008) and every year since they have an annual Jamboree to celebrate. They have musicians jamming in jam-packed streets. There's Jam in biscuits, Jam on toast, Jam on scones, Jam in tarts, traffic Jams, Jam roly-polys, toe Jam and they all wear py-jam-as.

It had a hugely positive impact; in fact, the Jam ripple was felt the world over, spreading a positive energy throughout the Empire. Prime Minister Bland changed the name of his country. As well as dropping the 'un' from Unkind, they also put a pot of Jam on the flag and changed their theme tune to 'Land of Cake and Glory'. As far as we know, they are all still living happily ever after.

No one really knows if this story is factually accurate or not but what we do know is this:

1. Grannies and cake make everything ok.
2. Saying nice things on the internet (and off it) might just change the world.

# dollop seven:

## How to train your parents

**Silliness Scale** 4

Questions that will bug your parents:

1. If you are in a spaceship that is travelling at the speed of light, and you turn on the headlights, does anything happen?

2. If we're not supposed to have midnight snacks, then why is there a light in the fridge?

3. What happens when you get half scared to death, twice?

4. Why are there life jackets under plane seats instead of parachutes?

5. When people lose weight, where the heck does it go?

6. Why are there no baby pigeons?

7. Why is it that 376% of people don't understand percentages?

# Welcome to the top Secretest club in the world

There are two types of adults; grown-ups and groan-ups. They're basically the same, but the second lot are a lot more negative. Your mission - should you choose to accept it (which you absolutely most definitely should btw) - is to train your parents so they maintain a positive attitude to life, work and parenting.

That's good for them but, more importantly, *it's much better for you.*

So we've started a secret club. It's a group of kids who are up for the challenge of training their parents, moulding their adults into something quite awesome. Because it was Gav's idea and Gav is Scottish, he didn't want to call it a club, he insisted on it being a clan. The Scots, they like a clan. 'Let's call it the "Can Clan"', he said, 'and our motto is "WE CAN!"'

So the '*WE CAN*' Can Clan was born.

Then we realised it's a secret club for kids to train their parents and Gav doesn't say 'kids', he says 'wee people', so we changed the name to the wee 'WE CAN' Can Clan.

So welcome to the wee '*WE CAN*' Can Clan. It's official.

You are now a member of it.

We're doing badges and everything.

**WE**
**CAN**
**Can Clan**

## Top secret insider knowledge

Parents. We've all got them; the big people who created the little people. They come in all sorts of shapes, colours and sizes. Large ones, small ones, curved ones and pointy ones. Some have hairy backs. Parents come with tattoos, some with piercings and some just plain. There are parents who stand-out and parents who blend in. Parents who have parents and parents who've had parents. There are even parents who are planning on being parents, again! But this time with a different parent.

Sometimes parents come in ones and sometimes they come in twos but nowadays families can become extended, like warranties and special Christmas tables. You can add step-parents, which creates step-sisters and step-brothers as well as step-grandparents.

All parents have two things in common. First up, they mean well and most of the time they get it just about right. Second - and this is something you never figure out as a kid - all parents are making it up as they go along.

Yes, ALL of them. And they're making EVERYTHING up as they go along. If you don't believe us, put the book down, and go ask, 'Dad, are you making your parenting skills up as you go along or have you got some sort of grand plan?'

## *See!*

This pressure leads to a whole array of parenting 'issues'. While you just crack on with growing up, your poor old folks start to fall apart. Obviously, you want fully functioning parents, right? If you want your meals serving at the right time, and your dirty socks washing and ironing, and your packed lunch packed and lunchy, and permission for sleepovers and whatnot - it's in your interest to get your parents ship shape and parenting-ready. So this is perhaps the most important section of a very important book about a super-important topic. This triple-importance rating means you have to read, EVERYTHING! absorb and DO everything in this dollop.

→

Remember, this is the key to YOU having as easy a life as possible.

Sit back and enjoy our wee *'WE CAN'* Can Clan top 10 tips on how to squeeze the very best out of your parent(s).

**FACT** alert.

'Dad' in German is spelt 'vater'. And they say the v like an F in German, that makes your dad a 'farter'.

Parents have more than enough on their plates but when it comes to eating, we mean literally! When it comes to eating and drinking, some parents have little self-control. They do not know when to say 'no'.

To keep your parents healthy, it's important to limit them to three good meals a day, with perhaps a few healthy snacks in between. What you put into your body affects what you get out. Good stuff in equates to an active, energetic and sparkly adult. Bad stuff in means they struggle to get off the sofa and fall asleep watching what is actually a really exciting detective series. So, if you want an attentive parent with a wet nose and shiny coat, always feed them sloooowly. Never fast. Fast food (like take-aways) goes in and out of the body too quickly and doesn't stick around long enough to do any good.

Start by suggesting that the 's' in 'fast food' should be a silent 's'. They probably won't get it because they're not as sharp as you. But it's still worth suggesting.

Insist they eat fruit and vegetables when they want to eat fruit and vegetables and even when they don't want to eat fruit and vegetables. If your parent is able to walk in a straight line on a Saturday night it's probably a sign that they have a balanced diet, which is good. If they fall over (which is bad) they might need to drink more water and less beer/wine.

Always remember, you are the child and therefore YOU are in charge of food. Your parents will eat what you eat so when they ask 'What do you want for tea?' make sure you give a *healthy* answer. Remember, these rules are about subtly influencing your parents, training them to be the best they can be so you get the best outcomes for you. So don't give a silly answer, otherwise they'll be onto you and the game's up. A silly answer to 'What do you want for tea?' is 'I'd love a plate of steamed broccoli and spinach please, mumpsy, on brown malted bread, with cous-cous, a side of edamame beans and a glass of freshly squeezed guava juice.'

See what we mean? That's too healthy. Brown bread gives it away and you'll be ousted as a member of the wee '*WE CAN*' Can Clan. Remember, once your parents suspect that you're training them, the game's up. Keep it real.

To keep your parents healthy the trick is for YOU to eat good food most of the time. Sure, you can treat your parents to a take-away or plasticky fast food thing *occasionally* - if they've behaved - but the general rule is to eat food that's nice to you and they will too. Good food for parents includes anything fresh and green (especially dark green), orange or purple. 'Whole' foods, so less processed, packaged and boxed. Help them out at the supermarket. Often, parents are so busy that they forget to read the labels. Make sure you have a quick look at what they're buying and always suggest a healthy alternative. Anything beige, sugary, fatty or fried is a 'no-no'.

Suggest your parent makes a few meals 'from scratch', which means they have to learn to put ingredients into a pan and create something wonderfully tasty and exciting. If they don't know what they're doing, sometimes it helps if YOU offer to help. There are plenty of healthy recipes on the internet. It's a well-known fact that if you cook for yourself, from scratch, it tastes so much better because you've invented it.

Please try and keep your parents off fizzy or energy drinks. The immediate high and low can be difficult for you to cope with. They will become hyper-active, badly behaved parents and then they'll experience a nosedive of feelings and slump in the corner. Again, please lead by example. Glug water, and plenty of it. Make sure they see you doing it. If they tell you water's boring tell them that their bodies are 85% water so they must be boring too. That usually shuts them up. In the long run, when they drink lots of water and their skin is shining, their brains un-fuddled and they are operating at maximum capacity, your parents will be brimming with good health and you will be on the receiving end of stellar parenting.

Oh, and one more thing. Always remember, parent training can be difficult. In terms of healthy eating you must never nag or whine. The trick is to make good suggestions about the family eating a healthy, balanced diet. If you keep at it, eventually the parent(s) will think that healthy eating and cooking from scratch and drinking lots of water was their idea and you can breathe a sigh of relief.

You report back to the wee *'WE CAN' Can Clan*. Job is done. The secret is safe.

Now, speaking of nagging ...

'Some people are
worth melting for.'
Olaf, Frozen

## Parenting rule #2:
## How to stop your parents nagging you.

Here's a fact you probably didn't know. When mums get diagnosed as 'pregnant' they're given a free book called 'How to nag your kid'. It's 100% compulsory that she reads it aloud to your dad, so he knows how to nag too. This 'How to nag your kid' book is top secret and made of bread, so they have to eat it after they've read it. That's why no child has ever seen 'How to nag your kid' lying around the house. There might be some crumbs, but no hard evidence.

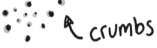 ← crumbs

So by the time you've reached, say, 7, or 10, they've had plenty of nagging practice. In the book they recommend that really experienced parents operate as a nag tag team. You, the child, get what's called 'repetitive ear injury' as they trot out the textbook 'Will you get off your computer please' and 'I won't ask you again: will you please do your homework.' Not forgetting the classics: 'You can't have any pudding unless you finish what's on your plate' and 'Will you please stop whining.' One of my mum's all time faves that she used to use on me like ALL the time when I was 8 was; 'Will you please stop flicking your sister's earlobes.' I would literally hear that 50 times on a rainy day as I sat and flicked my little sister's lobes and watched them wobble as she howled the house down.

Growing up, it can feel like you're living in Nag House, on Nag Street, Nagsville, being nagged by the nag tag team of Nagasaki.

Anyhow, the cure is simple. To cure yourself of repetitive ear injury - to literally STOP your parents asking you fifty times - here's the sneakiest thing a kid will ever learn ...

... do what they're asking, FIRST time!

It's super-cunning and works every single time. You'll find that your parent cures themself immediately, you get an easier life, and your little sister doesn't howl on a rainy day. Doing things on the first time of asking is, literally, the simplest and quickest and least painful way of training your parents. Oh, and it's really funny. Wait till you see the shock on their smug parenting faces as you literally DO WHAT YOU'RE TOLD, FIRST TIME, EVERY SINGLE TIME.

Sometimes they literally won't believe what's happening. Your mum will start saying 'Will you please eat...' and before she gets to '...your greens', they're gone. You've forked them in, swallowed, and have got your mouth open, wiggling your tongue, as proof. No fuss. No messing. Check the look on her face. The shock will be etched in and, most importantly, you've cut her off mid-nag.

Same with your dad. By the time he's finished the fatherly classic (it's the number 1 sentence in the 'How to nag your kid' bread book) 'Will you please stop annoying your sister and play nicely', you've stopped annoying your sister and are playing nicely. It's hilarious. It totally throws them because, you see, it doesn't tell them how not to nag in the bread book.

I'm not suggesting this works 99.9% of the time. It's a nailed on winning strategy - 100.1%.

There is a ninja level; if you can learn to do good stuff BEFORE they even have to ask you the first time then you'll enter the Hall of Fame at the wee *'WE CAN' Can Clan*. Your picture will be hanging on the wall in the grand-can-master Hall of Fame. If you ask us, there's probably a certificate for that. If not, when you ask us, we'll make one. To become a grand-can-master-parent-trainer you have to eat the veggies on your plate, do your homework, play nicely and not whine about small stuff so your parents don't even have to nag once. Just so you know, the grand-can-master Hall of Fame currently has no pictures hanging up. Maybe you could apply to be the first?

We interrupt this book to bring you an important interruption:

What do we want?

INTERRUPTING COWS!

When do we wan... 'MOO!'

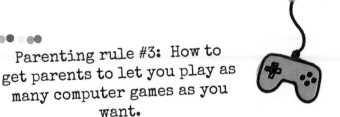

Parenting rule #3: How to get parents to let you play as many computer games as you want.

If you want unlimited freedom to play on your Nintendo-PSX-Sony-Microsoft-Switch-Box, you have to set a cunning parenting trap. First up, you have to negotiate a deal where an hour's extra gameplay is set as bait. You pitch it as a reward. Casually, of course. Throw a sentence into conversation along the lines of, 'Mumskins, you know if I come top of my spelling test tomorrow, could I be allowed a bit more screen time?'

No mumskins worth her salt will be able to resist the thought of her child being top of the class. If that happens, she'll be bragging to your grandma, the neighbours and it'll be posted all over FaceTok. She'll go for the bait every time. I mean, what mumskins wouldn't? Then you work like crazy, revise like a scientist, test yourself and nail next day's test. The results are counted, you're top of the class and BOOM! - you claim your cheeky prize.

## JOKE for no reason:

I went to the zoo yesterday and saw a baguette in a cage.

The zoo keeper told me it was bread in captivity.

Parenting rule #4:
How to get parents to let you have free,
unlimited ice-cream.

Exactly the same as the strategy above. You could vary the negotiation, for example, tidy your room, help make the tea, wash your mum's car, make cakes for your grandad. Any 'above and beyond' achievement will do. All you have to do is consistently go above and beyond and, hey presto, your parents will magically fall into line. Anything you want, becomes yours!

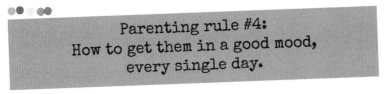

(The advanced ninja level is to negotiate unlimited fruit, broccoli and water. Admittedly, it's not quite as thrilling, but is a smart way of achieving rules 4 and 1 at the same time).

Parenting rule #4:
How to get them in a good mood,
every single day.

Again, this is *advanced* parenting training. Come closer. Listen in ...

Parents generally function pretty well during working hours of, say, 8am and 5pm. That's because, mostly, they're at actual work. But their happiness and energy at work doesn't benefit you. YOU need them happy and energetic outside working hours. Therefore, parents need pepping up at 7.30am and after 6pm.

At the wee `WE CAN` Can Clan we call it 'book ending' their day.

Here's how to train your parent to come alive in the morning ...

YOU come alive. I promise you, they'll follow. To guarantee a great start to the day, and to get your parents firing on all cylinders, why not have a go at the 4-minute rule. It's the smallest change that will have the biggest impact. The 4-minute rule basically says that it takes 4 minutes for other people to catch how YOU feel. So, to get your parents buzzing, all you have to do is be your best self for 4 minutes. How fab is that? You haven't got to be brilliant all day, just for the first 4 minutes of breakfast time and you'll have kick-started their day.

Obviously, you've figured out the problem here. How on earth do you get to be your best self first thing in the morning? You've crawled out of bed, you need a wee, and it's a Monday. None of those factors is particularly favourable.

The trick is to *not* have toothache.

Sounds weird, right? I know what you're thinking ... what on earth do you mean, the trick is to *not* have toothache. I haven't got toothache! So, when I wake-up I already don't have toothache.

*Exactly!*

The 'trick' is *celebrating* the fact that you've not got toothache. Let me explain it the opposite way around. Imagine if you *did* have toothache. If you've never had it, I promise you, toothache is proper miserable. It's a nagging pain that won't go away and the only solution is a trip to the dentist, which makes it doubly horrid. When names are called out in the dentist's waiting room nobody ever punches the air in celebration yelling, 'Yey, it's my turn!'.

Drills and whatnot. And that yucky pink liquid! What the heck even is that? A sticker for being good in no way compensates you for the suffering in that chair.

yucky pink liquid

So, every day that *doesn't* happen is brilliant news. Every day you wake-up and you *haven't* got toothache is a wonderful start to the day, which will put you in a fabulous mood. That means you'll be feeling amazing so by the time you've had your wee, got your school uniform on and made your way downstairs you will be bursting with positivity from *not* having toothache.

That means your first 4 minutes of family interaction is positive rather than grumpy and remember, the first 4 minutes is all it takes.

Warning – it's very easy to do the total opposite of the 4-minute rule. It's easy to forget that you've got to remember not to forget that you haven't got toothache. And if you forget to remember not to forget that you haven't got toothache, your first 4 family minutes will be just like every other household's first 4 minutes; bang average.

So, in order to guarantee bright and cheery parents first thing in the morning, get into the habit of celebrating that you haven't got toothache. Remember, your mum and dad need you to get their day off to a flyer.

But to bookend the day, you also need a tactic for the evening. There's no point playing the no-toothache card in the morning and then your parents wilting in an evening. So, when they ask you 'how was school?' - which they absolutely will, every single day of your school life - pep them up by giving a non-standard answer. That means blanking the blandness of 'fine' and 'okay'. Instead, pick out the highlight, and share that. Yes, even if they haven't even asked about the best thing, be determined to throw the best thing at them anyway. Remember, they're guaranteed to toss the lame 'how was your day?' question but just because they've asked a rubbish question, doesn't mean you have to stoop to a rubbish answer. Choose to upgrade. Pick out the best lesson, or the most amazing piece of learning or the funniest thing. And when you've shared the very best thing about your day - here's the kicker - ask what the highlight of *their* day was.

Try to look like you're interested. Put your active listening face on.

(It might be worth pausing for a practise because that's such an important face. Have a quick go at your 'active listening' face. *Look* like you're listening. If you're reading this book in class nudge the person next to you and show them your face. Ask them, 'What do you think I'm doing?' and if they say 'Listening', you've nailed it. That's the face! If they say 'You look like you're doing a poo', you've taken your active listening face too far. It's a common error. You're squeezing too hard basically, so come down a notch.)

Again, listening takes about 4 minutes, after which time your parents will be back in the game. The conversation will be positive. They will be beaming, their energy levels restored and you will receive parenting par-excellence.

Best of all, you've raised excellent parents.

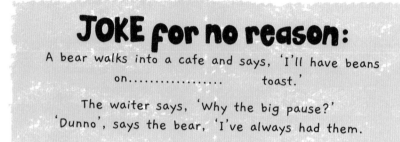

# JOKE for no reason:

A bear walks into a cafe and says, 'I'll have beans on................. toast.'

The waiter says, 'Why the big pause?'
'Dunno', says the bear, 'I've always had them.

You're a kid, so you understand that reading is good for you. It helps in so many ways. Not only in the obvious ways of boosting of your vocab and enhancing your ability to read and write, but being a good reader also sets you up to have a stellar life.

Like I say, you're clever. You already know that.

But sometimes parents can forget. They sometimes prefer to watch soap operas and detective series on the TV. Even worse, sometimes they develop a 'news habit' that causes them to shout at the TV. In time, their brains turn to mush. So, here's an interesting fact: the biggest factor in whether a parent reads or not is if they see their children reading. And the really interesting fact about that already interesting fact is that it applies to dads more than mums. So, if you're reading, your parents will likely switch off the news and open a book as well. If they don't, try suggesting that they do. Here's a sentence that usually works; 'Daddykins, I'm trying to read this wonderful book called "Brilliant Kid, The Big Number 2" (pause, he should laugh at that bit) but I'm struggling to concentrate because the telly's on and you're shouting at it. How about we switch the news off for 40 mins and both read a book together?'

Fathers are very simple creatures. Your idea seems perfectly reasonable and simple. Daddykins will give that 'good idea' nod that he sometimes does, but he might not have a book handy. So go and sit next to him and read him the rest of this dollop. Aloud. You do a page, he does a page, and so on. You can help him with the difficult bits.

If you do it for 40 minutes a day and keep it up for 21 days, it will become a habit. Your dad will start to expect you and him to read together. It's actually rather sweet and is a sure-fire way of improving your parents' intelligence and vocabulary without them realising you're in total control.

Even better news - when you congratulate your dad on his impeccable behaviour, he'll know what impeccable means.

## Parenting rule #7:
### How to get your parents to be super-calm and non-shouty.

Adults go to bed late and get up early, despite telling you to go to bed early and get up late. This means they can spend a large part of the day feeling a bit cranky. Don't take it personally, your parent is just pushing the boundaries. It's called the 'naughty thirties.' To put your parent in a better mood, it's important that they get into good sleep habits. So here are some top tips on how to train your parents to get good kip.

Suggest that nobody in the family uses their phone from 7pm onwards. Screen time wakes you up rather than putting you to sleep so if everyone's scrolling or playing on their console, nobody will feel sleepy at sleep time. Your cunning ploy is to suggest the family sit together and chill with an hour's family TV before bedtime. That's all of you together in the same room, watching the same thing. Monday to Thursday is a series that you all enjoy. Friday and Saturday are family movie nights. Sunday is a wildlife documentary because it gets your parents' brains sharpened for work tomorrow.

Remember, documentaries are like broccoli for the mind.

Then at 8pm you volunteer to go to bed to set a good example. No fuss. Please be consistent about this. Go brush your teeth, put your jimjams on, come and give them a peck on the cheek and say night-night. If they question your superb behaviour tell them that children of your age need 9 or 10 hours of sleep to be fully functioning. Remind them that fully functioning adults need at least 8 hours. Tell them that they've been good parents so you're letting them stay up till 9pm to watch an extra programme ... but they need to go to bed, no fuss, after that.

**Be firm!** You don't want grumpy-chops parents!

Also, suggest that they leave their phones outside their bedroom at night. Otherwise, all of those 'alerts', will leave them feeling anything but alert the following morning. Say this: 'Mum, Dad, it's a BED-room. The clue is in the name of the room. Like BATH-room is for having a bath, DINING-room is for dining and KITCHEN ... hang on, that last one doesn't work. But a BED-room has a BED in it, for sleeping.'

One last thing on training your parents for sleep ... always go to bed happy. If your parent has been naughty, make sure that you let them know tomorrow is a new day and a fresh start.

## Fact-advice

# Sleep literally cleans your brain. So go to bed early!

All parents occasionally act without thinking or think without acting. Sometimes, when they are sat in traffic, for instance, they can go red and start repeating unrepeatable words - particularly if it's a very long traffic jam. We won't repeat any of the unrepeatable words here, and neither should you. If they say bad things, give them the eyebrow. You know the one; the warning eyebrow. (Again, that's worth practising either with a partner or in front of the mirror. It involves raising a single eyebrow. If you raise both, that's 'surprise' and, remember, you're supposed to be giving a stern warning. If you don't know how to do it, ask your teacher. They have 'warning eyebrow' training as part of their teaching practice.)

On super-long holiday journeys, the only rule of how to train your parents is never ever ask 'Are we nearly there yet', as it nearly always makes matters worse. Their answer is always 'No, we've not even got off the driveway yet!'

Instead, spend the journey being patient and nice. Ask those in the front seats to tell you about the holidays they used to have as a kid. That makes the journey seem quicker for them and you can get some sleep while they're droning on and on about caravanning in Cornwall.

'A two-year-old
is kind of like
having a blender,
but you don't have
a top for it.'

Jerry Seinfeld

Sometimes parents don't want to go to work, especially
not on a Monday. This is called a career. Those who
haven't got a career have got an even harder job.
They've made a career out of giving up their other
career to look after you.

You are their career! *Imagine?*

They've given up their pay, to work for you, for free. They
are basically your servant. It's guaranteed that whatever
job they were doing before - cage fighting, wrestling with
wild yak, walking on hot coals - will have been an easier
career than the one that they have right now.

When they start hating Mondays, it needs nipping-in-the-bud before their Blue Monday feeling starts to creep into Sunday night. Mondays are just as much of a day as any other day but have a lot of unkind words directed towards them. Parents need to learn to be nicer to Mondays, and Mondays will, in turn, be nicer to them. That way every day is a winner and everyone wins every day. The trick to getting your school week off to a flyer is to hatch a plan to get your parents to fall in love with Mondays. This isn't easy, because literally everyone hates Mondays. That means you have to be different to literally everyone.

Here's the trick.

At school you are taught about equality, diversity and fairness. You also have an anti-bullying policy. And yet the world continues to mistreat Mondays. Obviously, we don't need to convince you of the value of Mondays. You are clever enough to have figured out that YOU SPEND A SEVENTH OF YOUR ENTIRE LIFE ON MONDAY so that's too big a chunk to waste. But for adults, who have less life left, Mondays can lose their sparkle. Your parents will often be happier on any day other than Monday. Remember, this Monday slump is not good for them, or you. Scientists have been studying it and children have been wrestling with 'grumpy Monday syndrome' since children were first invented, back in 1971.

At last, we can reveal the answer to this most basic

of problems. How to rid your parents of their Monday slump is to sit them down on Sunday evening and explain about bullying.

Here's how the discussion should go, approximately ... 'Mummykins, Daddy-o, hypothetically, if I was being bullied at school what would you do?'

Daddy-o will all-of-a-sudden clench his right fist (left, if he's left-handed), his eyes will get big and he'll ask, 'Who is it? You've gotta stick up for yourself, kiddo. Punch 'em right back. That's watcha gotta do ....'

That's really bad advice - but you already know that. The point is that your parents have stepped right into your cunning trap.

'No parent-poops, I'm not being bullied. Mondays, they're the ones being kicked around. The haters are out there doing what the haters do, and I'm worried about Monday. So, I've decided to set up a petition called "Stand Up for Mondays." Looky here.' (At this point you pull the petition from your pocket and show them. It doesn't need to be anything fancy. Just a piece of A4 with 'Petition' written on the top, although if you can draw a grid on it that adds to the effect.)

'I've already got one signature - mine - and I need some more. So, if you are anti-bullying, will you please sign my petition?'

You see how it works? *Everyone* is anti-bullying. Even bullies! So they can't NOT sign the 'Stand Up for Mondays' petition. Next day, which happens to be Monday, the petition is in full view on the kitchen table and they won't have a bad word to say.

This is a level of genius that most parents never reach and, again, the best thing is that you have trained the old dogs to learn new tricks (perhaps best NOT tell them they're 'old dogs', otherwise all your good deeds will be undone).

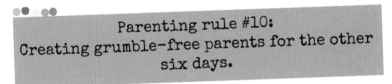

Parenting rule #10:
Creating grumble-free parents for the other six days.

This top parenting tip is all about language because the words you use are super-powerful. So, to give your parent the best start in life, use nice words. The general rule is that you should be six times more positive than you are negative.

Let me explain. Every time you whinge or grumble or criticise or complain or say 'it's not fair', you should say SIX positives to compensate.

Yes, SIX (6)!

That means you need to look out for chances to catch your parents doing something well, and tell them. Here are some examples:

'Mum, this sandwich is dee-lish-us.'

'Dad, your hair looks super-amazing.'

'Mum, thank you for washing my PE kit.'

'Popsies, I love the way you read me that bedtime story. You're the best dad in the world.'

'Mumski, you've got the loveliest smile.'

'Daddykins, you make the world's most amazing mashed potatoes. I love the way you don't actually hardly mash them at all so they've got lumps in. In fact, you're genius at basically squashing potatoes.'

You get the idea. Don't make a big deal of it. Don't be silly about it. Don't let them know what you're up to. We absolutely promise, if you catch them doing things well and tell them, they will repeat said behaviours. Hey presto, you get more delicious sandwiches, shiny PE kit, super bedtime stories and lumpy mashed potato.

It all boils down to this; actions speak louder than words. But words sometimes speak pretty loudly too. Especially if you shout them. Therefore, actions AND words are important.

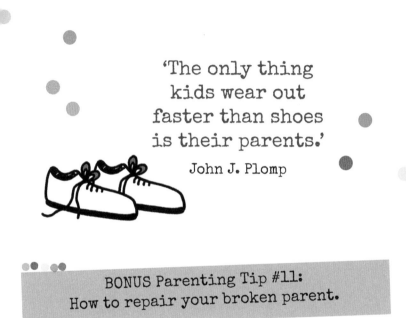

'The only thing
kids wear out
faster than shoes
is their parents.'

John J. Plomp

BONUS Parenting Tip #11:
How to repair your broken parent.

'Always under-promise and over-deliver' is almost a point in its own right. That's what we've done here, see. We promised 10 top parenting tips and we've only gone and added an 11th. That's 10% extra free and everyone likes 10% extra free, unless you're buying hassle.

Underneath it all a parent is actually a human being. They're built to certain specifications so are able to withstand the normal wear and tear of life. But remember, the pressures are considerable. Not only keeping food on the table and a roof over the family's head, but also paying bills, having a job and squeezing in time to go to the pub. Therefore, sometimes they do actually break - and that's fine.

Parents don't come with a receipt. If your parent is wilting under the strain, or if they have developed a fault, or have actually broken, you can't take them back to the shop and swap them for a new one. But here's a sure-fire 100% guaranteed way to help fix a broken parent.

You must put the love back into their hearts. It's two strategies, actually.

In fact, three:

First, if it was you who caused them to break, say sorry and mean it. That will help you and them to move on and put whatever 'it' was behind you. And that's where you need to leave all your troubles - in the past.

Second, if it wasn't you that caused them to be on a downer, it was just 'life' generally, tell them you love them and mean it.

↑ **LOVE**
**repair**
**kit** ×

The third thing in your love repair kit is to administer a magical 7-second hug. Note, the average hug lasts 2.1 seconds so 7 seconds is really stretching it. Which is exactly the point. Sometimes your parents need a pick-me-up so a 7-second hug, plus an 'I love you' and/or 'I'm sorry' and mean it! It's a wonderful explosion of love that heals almost anything. My daughter did it to me and my athlete's foot cleared up the very same day.

(Warning: when administering a 7-second hug, don't count out loud. It spoils the effect. Oh, and just so you know, you don't actually have to wait for your parent to look jaded before you do the 7-second hug thing. They provide an instant boost pretty much anytime. If you don't believe me, put the book down, go do a 7-second hug and report back.)

'It's a funny thing about mothers and fathers. Even when their own child is the most disgusting little blister you could ever imagine, they still think that he or she is wonderful.'

Matilda by
Roald Dahl

*Phew!* It's been a long dollop so here's a summary of the parenting rules of the wee *'WE CAN' Can Clan*. We're thinking of setting up another wee *'WE CAN' Can Clan*, but in Kazakhstan. In fact, we see these wee *'WE CAN' Can Clan* 'brilliant parenting' clubs springing up in the most unlikely of places; Iran, Japan, Amsterdam, Milan

...

That way it becomes a global movement of brilliant parenting, created by the kids, for the kids.

Here's your reminder. Follow these rules and you will create parents that obey your every command:

1. Feed them healthy food and lots of water. Remember, they will copy whatever they see you doing, so teach them well.

2. To stop them nagging make sure you do everything first time of asking.

3. To get unlimited computer time simply suggest it as 'bait' – a reward for any extra mile activity – then simply go the extra mile. Hey presto, the reward is yours!

4. This also works for unlimited ice-cream.

**5. Top and tail their day with positivity.** That means the 4-minute rule in the morning and asking them about the highlight of their day in the evening.

**6.** To improve your parents' vocabulary read to them for 40 minutes every day.

**7.** Nobody likes shouty parents so reduce their stress by insisting on good sleeping habits.

**8.** On long car journeys, keep your parents in tip-top condition by never asking 'Are we nearly there yet?'

**9.** For marvellous Mondays play the sneaky anti-bullying card. Have them sign up to your 'Stand Up for Mondays' petition.

**10.** To create a positive family, remember actions and words both speak loudly. Make both count. Every grumble needs repairing with SIX positives.

**11. BONUS TIP:** To fix a broken parent you have three tools in your love repair kit:
a. If it was you who broke them, say sorry *and mean it.*
b. If it was 'life' that broke them, tell them you love them *and mean it.*
c. If they look like they need pepping up administer an emergency 7-second hug *and mean it.*

Finally, parents are, by and large, simple creatures. Remember, they are taller and therefore the air they breathe is thinner due to the increased altitude. That explains their light-headedness. This means they can sometimes become a little dizzy so they don't always make the best decisions - or even the right decisions.

Fortunately, they're easily led, so LEAD THEM.
By your good example.

Most of the time, that will work.

But if you lead by good example and they *still* don't follow then the only tactic left is fear. Remember, this final top tip is for when you've tried rules 1 to 11 and they're still not obeying your every command.

Our *bonus* bonus parenting tip (we are now giving you 20% extra free) is this - simply scare the living daylights out of them by suggesting that one day they're going to be really really really old and it'll be YOU who's choosing which care home they go into. Put on your sternest face, your waggiest finger, and say this: 'If you don't start behaving RIGHT NOW I'll be selecting a shoddy place, with a scary nurse, a bad cook and a lounge that smells of wee.'

'You're mad. Bonkers. Off your head... But I'll tell you a secret... ...some of the BEST people are

Alice (in Wonderland)

# dollop eight:

## The ULTIMATE poetry challenge

Silliness scale **9**

Dollop 7 was big, important and long, so we're rewarding you with something small, silly and short.

Here comes a poem called 'The Selfish Shellfish'. It's got a wellbeing moral, but sometimes poems aren't about what they're actually about. Sometimes they're not about the meaning of the words, they're about the saying of the words.

And saying words can be so much fun.

So please accept our challenge. You'll need a phone with a stopwatch because we're asking you to time yourself. Your mission is to read 'The Selfish Shellfish' as quickly as you can. If you stumble, or get a word wrong, you go back to the start of the line you stumbled on.

That's the only rule. Unless 'no cheating' is a rule, in which case there are two.

The current world record is 76.88 seconds.

Post your efforts online (that might be a third rule?).

Good luck.

You're going to need it, Selfish Shellfish sucker!

# The Selfish Shellfish

Shelley was a shellfish. A swell fish. But, truth be known, she was a selfish shellfish.

She was married to the very unselfish Seth Shellfish.
(He'd lost a claw in a fishing incident)

For Seth the unselfish shell-shocked shellfish, life was hellish.

Seth was an unwell unselfish shellfish.

Shelley Shellfish's hobby was selfies.

So, yes, Shelley was a selfish selfie-taking shellfish.
(Relax, here comes the easy bit ...)

She pouted and posed and smiled and preened.

And puckered and frowned and posted to
screen. Shelley Shellfish's selfies were dark.
She wanted more light.

So Shelley the selfie-taking selfish shellfish made a wish.

She left Seth, her unwell unselfish
shell-shocked shellfish, and moved somewhere
more swish.

Where the light was fantastic!

Her selfies were something that Shelley Shellfish
could cherish.

Felt cute, might delete later
x

**BUT...** the selfish shellfish was selfying so hard that
she failed to see ...

And was scooped from the pool, *oh deary me!*

Selfish Shelley, the selfie shellfish would perish.

That night in the cafe the humans agreed, the selfish shellfish was indeed a swell fish.

Shelley had ended up on a dish.

Totes delish!

(With a squeeze of lemon and radish and relish)
*Shish!* She was totes delish.

(Please share your readings online using #SelfishShellfish. Remember, you're aiming to beat 76.88 seconds).

# dollop nine:

## Joe's Amazing Technicolour Wheelie-Bin

3

Silliness Scale

# You'll need crayons and felt tips

Great Uncle Joe wasn't very good at being happy. He'd mastered grumbling, frowning and cursing under his breath, but happiness wasn't really a strength. Life, to Joe, was rubbish. It was rubbish on a Tuesday, it was rubbish on a Friday, and it was especially rubbish on a Monday. The other days in-between weren't great either. He was even straight-faced on a Saturday, which shows you just how expert Great Uncle Joe had become at making a hash of his life.

Life, for Joe, was one big pile of rotting, stinking, fermenting, maggot-ridden rubbish.

He'd got deeply entrenched in a habit if grumpiness, which was curious because he hadn't always been like that. He'd *learned* to be like that.

Great Uncle Joe     Harriet Sweet-Tooth

The old chap lived next door to Harriet Sweet-Tooth. She was absolutely lovely, very sweet, with not a single grumpy bone in her body. In fact, her body was quite squashy. Harriet liked puddings you see. She also liked Great Uncle Joe, and would sometimes offer him a cake, or a fruit crumble, but he always refused. Now, this was odd, because even when Great Uncle Joe was telling his neighbour that he didn't want any cake he knew it wasn't true. He loved cake! And crumble, and trifle and rice pudding. But his negativity had got so ingrained that he couldn't stop refusing happy things, even when they were offered to him on a plate.

Or, indeed, in a dish.

Great Uncle Joe's lowlight of the week was on a Tuesday evening, when he could grumpily trundle his 240 litre, dreary grey wheelie-bin all the way down the length of his rubbish weed-riddled driveway. There it would stand all night, full to the brim of Joe's rotting, stinking, fermenting, maggot-ridden rubbish - plus a little more besides - until the bin wagon rocked up and a week's worth of rottenness was driven away.

Sometimes he also wheeled Mrs Harriet Sweet-Tooth's bin as well.

Please read that bit again because it's a clue. A BIG clue!

Yes, Great Uncle Joe was grumpy, but there was still some niceness inside. There was a glimmer of hope. His happiness was hidden, not just from his neighbours, but from himself.

Bin day is Wednesday, so please imagine it's now early morning on Thursday. Still a little bit dark. The bin wagon has done its thing and trundled to the next street.

Great Uncle Joe traipsed down the length of his driveway expecting to collect his newly emptied dreary grey wheelie-bin. He could then fill it to the brim with rotting, stinking, fermenting, maggot-ridden rubbish – plus a little more besides – all over again. Standing in front of him, however, was no longer an ordinary grey bin. It was simply the most spectacular bin that you ever did see, covered in stripes of every colour and bedecked with gold and silver stars that twinkled brightly. The bin was almost, but not quite, glowing.

It was Joe's Amazing Technicolour Wheelie-Bin.

Great Uncle Joe was puzzled. He rattled his bin and it felt full. His first instinct was to grumble that the bin men had forgotten to empty his stinking rotten rubbish because they were good-for-nothing employees of the local stinking rotten council. As he was halfway through that thought he flipped the lid (the bin's lid, not his) and got the fright of his life. A golden ray of sunshine, about as powerful as a lighthouse, beamed into the early morning sky. He shielded his eyes and ears as the happiest song he'd ever heard boomed from the bin. Great Uncle Joe leapt at the bin and closed the lid, cutting off the light and music show. The old man frowned, his wrinkles falling into a familiar pattern.

Assuming the council had delivered him a faulty bin, he trundled it back to his house, where he'd lodge a formal complaint and perhaps get some sort of compensation. He wanted his rubbish rubbish bin back.

He huffed and puffed and heaved and weaved his way back along the gravel driveway and all the way to his back door. His bin was 'evidence' that the council had messed up so he thought he'd better wheel it indoors for safe-keeping. He opened the door and levered the bin inside, where it stood radiantly in the middle of the kitchen floor, like a rubbish bin sent from the heavens.

For some time, Joe sat looking at his bin and the bin sat looking back at Joe until he did the only thing that he could do; he opened the bin for another sneaky peek. The moment he lifted the lid, sunlight engulfed the kitchen, filling the room with bright yellow warmth. The happy song rang out, far too loud for this time of day. Shielding his eyes with one hand, Joe reached into the bin and pulled out the first thing he clasped – an old pair of dancing shoes – and slammed the lid shut.

Joe looked at them in the silence of his kitchen. His reflection peered back from their buffed patent leather toes. They were black and white and looked somehow familiar. He tentatively slipped them on to his feet and experienced a Binderella moment [4]. They were a perfect fit! Immediately, Joe felt the urge to slide and pirouette around the flag-stoned floor. He leapt and jumped and twisted and twirled, puffing and smiling and whooping with delight. He stood-up straighter than he had in years and his knees were perhaps a little less creaky.

He foxtrotted from the kitchen to the lounge before tangoing back again. He tap-danced on the kitchen tiles until he could dance no more. Great Uncle Joe paused for breath and caught his reflection in the cooker hood. The deep furrows upon his brow seemed somehow not quite so deep anymore. Joe's eyes grew wide and twinkled; he could feel something he had not done in a very long time. He wasn't sure what the feeling was, but he liked it!

[4] Like a Cinderella moment but it involves bins

The old man couldn't resist delving into the bin once more. Shielding his eyes and wrapping a scarf around his ears, Joe reached in and this time he grappled with something a bit bigger. He had to bend right in and wrestle the thing from the depths of the Amazing Technicolour Wheelie-Bin, keeping his eyes tight shut to shield them from the golden rays.

Lid shut, scarf lowered, he saw an easel, some paints and brushes. 'Oh my goodness,' he smiled aloud. 'I remember that paint set!' As a child and young adult Joe had loved to paint. In fact, he'd been a very good artist, especially landscapes and seasides and nature. Great Uncle Joe was grinning like a cat from a county toward the northwest of England. Now he had a brand-new paint set, he vowed, there and then, to kick-start his hobby.

The old chap fancied one more dip into the bin; this time he wore his sunglasses and earmuffs so he could have a longer rummage. He also put factor 40 sun-cream on because of the rays. The kitchen was flooded with light and any neighbours who weren't awake, were now, as the 'Hallelujah Chorus' made his house shake. Great Uncle Joe's feet were peeking out of the Amazing Technicolour Wheelie-Bin as he leaned in and had a good feel around.

He emerged with a dog-eared full-colour cookbook, entitled 'Mrs Kipling's Exceedingly Good Buns, Cakes, Puddings and Desserts'. Leafing through the pages,

he licked his lips as recipe after recipe of chocolate treats and caramel tarts whetted his appetite. He used to love baking. He used to love eating what he'd baked. These days Uncle Joe only ate beans on toast, and sometimes beans under toast. His finger settled on 'Sticky Toffee Pudding', an old favourite of Joe's. After scurrying around the pantry and collecting some dusty tins and out-of-date ingredients he set about making the pudding with wild abandon.

A short while later the golden-brown sticky toffee pudding sat looking at Joe, very sticky and very toffee-ee. He was going to tuck right in but he remembered that Mrs Sweet-Tooth, from next door, liked puddings. With a smile on his face he waltzed out of his front door, hurdled the hedge and rat-a-tat-tatted on Mrs Sweet-Tooth's knocker. The old lady was delighted to be invited. 'Sticky toffee pudding for breakfast,' she cooed, her mouth slobbering and her eyes spinning. 'Give me 10 minutes,' she beamed, 'and I'll come over with custard.'

Returning to the technicolour wheelie-bin, Joe rummaged around once more, and this time pulled out a large square book. Opening the cover, he realised it was filled with photographs. It was a family photograph album crammed full of pictures of birthdays, sports days, holidays and away days, football games, cricket matches, fun in the sun and holiday mayhem. There were grandmas and grandkids and stepbrothers and little sisters and long-forgotten best friends. There were snapshots of laughing and dancing and mishap and good fortune; small people and big people and babies that are no longer babies and grown-ups that ...

... are no longer.

*Gulp!*

Joe looked at the pictures of great nephews and nieces. He wondered how old they were now and right there and then Joe vowed to put the 'great' back into Great Uncle Joe.

Yes, it had been too long, but it wasn't too late. The doorbell rang and Mrs Sweet-Tooth smiled her way in, carrying a large jug of steaming custard. The pair ate, and danced, right there in the kitchen. The next day they went to the park. Saturday, they went roller skating, and the day after that they went to the seaside, to exactly the same place as in the old photo album. Mrs

Sweet-Tooth marvelled as Great Uncle Joe did the best seaside painting ever.

Oh, and in case you're wondering, this story does have a happy ending. The magic wheelie-bin had reminded Joe what he wanted to be for the rest of his days.

He wanted to be happy. And that required a very special type of magic.

Everyday magic.

Great Uncle Joe and Mrs Sweet-Tooth became a happy couple. Joe wrote to the council thanking them for being so epic. The council moved Joe's Amazing Technicolour Wheelie-Bin to Mrs Frownalot's bungalow at number 56. Great Uncle Joe and Mrs Sweet-Tooth lived happily ever after, with lashings of custard.

# Activity:

Life is, on the whole, a pretty marvellous affair. But when the grumbles set in – which they will occasionally do – the everyday magic is a simple reminder of things that make you feel amazing. A daily dose of magical memories.

Imagine you have your very own Amazing Technicolour Wheelie-Bin. First of all, you're feeling the need to draw it, right? So here's an entire page for you to create the most amazing wheelie-bin the council has ever seen. Beyond anyone's imagination. Even Mrs Frownalot won't be able to help herself! Be sure to draw the words and tune blasting out.

Once it's drawn, what would you like to pull out of it? What five things or memories or people or pets or smells or clothes or games would remind you of amazing times in your life? If one day you were sad, what would turn that frown upside down?

# dollop ten:

## Chip 'n' Pin:
## The Money Savvy Kids™

Financial advice from the UK's penny-pinching twins

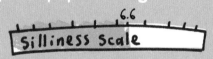

6.6

Silliness Scale

Dear Chip 'n' Pin, **The Money Savvy Kids**™
My mummy says money doesn't grow on trees.
Is this true or is there actually some sort of
money rainforest that I can go to and pick my
own notes?
Yours financially,
Armitage Shanks (age 1)

Dear Armitage,

There is actually something called a 'money tree' which I've just Googled. From the pictures on the internet it doesn't look like there's money hanging from it but I'm guessing that if you planted enough of them they might one day evolve into some sort of money rainforest.

Or – and this is me thinking aloud – if you planted a pound coin it might eventually decompose and turn into soil and a tree could grow in that exact spot and it could have pound coin fruit?

If that was the case, you might be better off planting a £20 note because then the fruit would be worth more.

TBH Armitage, I'm guessing. But it could happen. Evolution is quite slow, so if money trees do evolve to grow actual money it's going to take millions of years so meantime, I'm afraid the answer is no.

Yours financially,
Chip (the 2-minute older twin. Older and wiser!)

# Reader's email

Dear Chip 'n' Pin, The Money Savvy Kids™

My daddy says 'Money can't buy happiness' but, surely, it can? He bought himself a new car last week and he sure seems a lot happier. Same with my mummy and shoes.
Yours financially,
Splendid Patel (age 9)

What a splendid question, Splendid. The 'can money buy happiness' conundrum goes to the heart of a debate that's been swilling around for a fair old while. It's a long answer but if I butcher it to the bare bones it's this: Your dad is talking nonsense. Yes, money can buy happiness. BUT only if you spend it on the right things. Generally speaking, here are the rules on how to squeeze max value from your happiness pound:

*1. You'll get more happiness from experiences rather than products. That means trips to the zoo, seaside, football matches, etc.*

*2. If you absolutely have to buy a product buy something that lets you have an experience – so a bike, skateboard, magic set, guitar, new rugby ball, swimming trunks, tennis racket, etc.*

*3. Spending money on other people will generally earn you more happiness points than spending it on yourself. Yes, it's weird, but true. You don't have to spend ALL your pocket money on other people but if you occasionally buy your sister an ice-cream or your dad a bunch of flowers, that will make them and you very happy.*

*One more thing, Splendid. Money is absolutely NOT a happiness guarantee. For example, there are a lot of rich people who are unhappy and quite a few poor ones who are happy. Rather than investing in money, you will be better off investing in relationships. Close friendships and a nice family – these will make you happier than money.*

*Yours commercially,*
*Pin (the slightly younger twin, so I'll probably live longer)*

### Reader's social media post

 @BlueYonder44

Dear Chip 'n' Pin, **The Money Savvy Kids™**
My mum keeps on grumbling about the electricity and gas bills. They keep going up apparently. How can I make them go down?

---

 @Chip_n_Pin

Dear @BlueYonder44
Want extra pocket money? Ask you parents to show you the electricity and gas bills. Tell them that if the next bills are lower than the current bills, YOU get to keep the difference. They'll agree, thinking this will never happen. For the next 6 months you are super careful to switch lights off and read books instead of playing on electricity-heavy games consoles. You also wear an extra jumper and switch the heating down a notch. Star jumps in the morning are a good way to warm you up.

Bingo, by the end of the year you will be £34.77 richer and you've become more 'environmentally friendly'. The environment is now friends with you.

Yours economically,
Chip the elder

Chip 'n' Pin, **The Money Savvy Kids**™

*Top money-making tip*
*Need extra cash for school dinners or to treat your mates*
*to a meal deal? Simply set up an eBay account and auction*
*your little brother off. You can often get somewhere*
*between £4 and £6.*

*Yours creatively,*
*Pin (I've actually tried this but unfortunately Chip's still*
*here!)*

Reader's email

Dear Chip 'n' Pin, The Money Savvy Kids™

I really want one of those new games consoles. And
then I also want lots of really expensive games to go
with the console. Oh, and a brand-new top of the range
smartphone. But my family doesn't have any money. My
mom is always complaining that she has three part-
time jobs to make ends meet. What should I do?
Anxia Whiny-Voice (age 8)

Dear Anxia,
You should read this book instead. That way, you'll
become super positive, be a lovely person, get good
grades, find a superb job, earn lots of money and
then lend your parents some of it because they are
wonderful parents. Please cut them some slack. They
love you so much it hurts.

Yours truthfully,
Chip 'n' Pin's money savvy mom

Dear Chip 'n' Pin, The Money Savvy Kids™
My mum says I should walk to school but I
prefer to drive. What should I do?
Morgan Toyota (age 6)

Dear Morgan,
You are six for goodness sake! That's
nowhere near old enough to drive. Please
walk. It saves the hassle of parking, it's good
for you, it saves petrol, it saves the planet
and there's much less chance of you getting
arrested.

Yours road-safely,
Pin 'n' Chip (swapped it because I'm sick of
always being mentioned second)

# dollop eleven:

## Daymares[5]

```
    3           6
  |  |  |  |  |  |  |  |
  | Silliness scale      |
  3, rising to 6 in places
```

[5] Apols. Not feeling it today. Couldn't think of any words.
Please move on.

Whoops, here's a totally blank page[6]

[6] Again! Sorry. Second bad day on the bounce. Hopefully there will be some words tomoz. If not, you might like to think about claiming a refund. Try this as a letter starter: 'Dear publisher. I bought your Brill Kid Big Number 2 (still funny btw) but there were some blank pages. Total white-outs. It might be that your printer cartridge ran out or it could be that the authors couldn't think of anything to write. And that illustrator lady couldn't even be bothered to draw a picture. This is not how books should be. Please post my refund to [insert your address].

# A letter for the worriers

Dear Worriers,

Gav here. *Phew!* Feeling much better today. Thanks for asking. Words flow so much better when I'm feeling amazing. To be fair, *everything* seems a whole lot easier when I'm feeling amazing! Life is so much more do-able.

But nobody feels amazing all the time. Except dogs, maybe?

Life sometimes gets in the way. Even happy people get sad. Everyone's allowed an off day. The trick is to bounce back stronger.

I'd love to share something with you that up until a few years ago was top secret! I'm only going to tell you though on the basis you don't laugh.

So here goes. *Pssst*, come closer. I'm whispering.

*I worry about things.*

Yeah, probably not the big, exciting secret you were hoping for! You see, the thing is, I worry about a lot of things, a lot of the time. And sometimes it can get a bit much and I feel overwhelmed by my worries. Then I start to worry about the fact I'm worrying!

That's right, I'm 41, I'm married, I have two kids, I run my own business, I write books, I've performed stand-up comedy all over the world and yet, I worry about things.

You might have heard it called 'anxiety' or 'stress' but those terms are incorrect. The technical term for my condition is called 'being human'. And guess what? We're all human. Here's a cool fact for you, worrying is normal. Doubts and anxieties are normal too.

Knowing these worrying thoughts are normal doesn't stop me having them. My anxiety explains the two blank pages. It stops me in my tracks.

If there was a job 'professional worrier' I'd be the boss man. I've had a lifetime of practice. I've been a worrier since I was about 2 years old. Here's some of the things I've worried about in my life.

Doing poos

Falling down the toilet

The dark

Being alone

Being in groups

Thunder

Heights

Being ill

The doctor

Hospitals

Flying

Plane crashes

Escalators

Lifts

School

My gran's beard

Reading out loud in class

Being trapped in a hole

Hospitals (so worried about this that I've included it twice)

Geese (swans too, actually. Ducks less so)

Horses

Bullies

War

My body

The way I look

My friends

What people think of me

What people don't think of me

Being alone

Being in groups

hole

Exams
Failing
Succeeding
Panicking that my alarm won't go off and
I'll be late for work
Stressing that I'll forget to get dressed and
rock up at work in my pjs and slippers
Girls
Boys
Getting old
Getting stuck in a lift
Dying (while trapped in a lift)
Living (while trapped in a lift)
My job
Not having my job
Paying bills
Going bald
Sprouting purple armpit hair
People called Gerald
Not worrying

That last one's weird, right? Imagine being
worried about not worrying? I do that!
Sometimes I have random days when I have
nothing to worry about and I worry that
tomorrow might throw *double* worry at me. I
can hear tomorrow's booming voice; 'I'll teach
you to NOT worry. Just you wait!'

See, that's why I'm the boss man of
worrying. I'm *that* good!

If you study my list you'll see there are some things on there that are definitely not worth worrying about but through life it's hard to predict what kind of things will lead to worrying.

Talk!

I've learned that the best thing to do if you're worried about something is talk to someone about it. I know everyone says that but it's true. Talk to your parents, grandparents, friends, teachers or even your pets! Worries are generally secret. We keep them to ourselves. As soon as the secret's out, some of the worry disappears, too.

I often find that most things I worry about turn out to be ok in the end.

Here's an example of a true worry story...

What do we want?

LOW FLYING AIRPLANE NOISES!

WHEN DO WE WANT'EM?

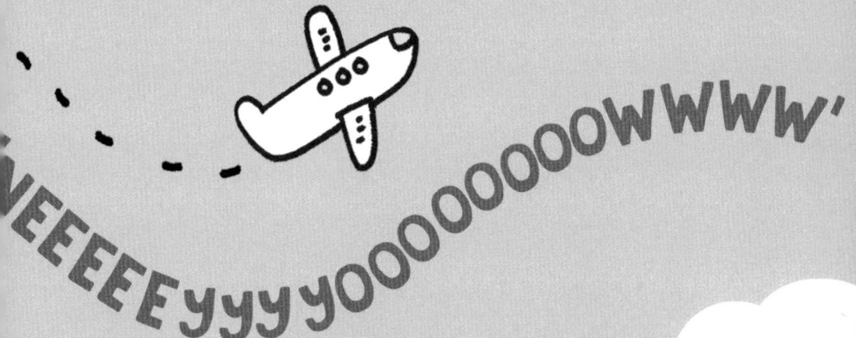

# Stage Fright!

A few years ago I was invited to speak at what's called a TEDx event. Now, if you've never heard of a TEDx event it's a pretty big deal where you do a talk to a crowd of people, everyone brings their A-game and it's filmed so millions of people watch it. This one was especially special as it was to be held at St Andrews University, one of the most prestigious universities in the world. I was buzzing, couldn't wait to get on that stage and do my thing.

The theme for the day was all around play and rediscovering your inner child. *Perfect!*

I wanted to try something completely different. I decided my talk would be all about why so many grown-ups don't play anymore, and I wanted to come up with something that would prove it. What could I do in a lecture theatre with 300 grown-ups?

There's no way I could play Hide 'n' Seek, that would be crazy. No one would ever do that. Plus, it could never work in that kind of space. Remember, I'm on stage in a theatre. There's nowhere to hide! So, because it was a stupid idea that would never work, my decision was made.

*Hide 'n' Seek it was.*

To set the scene quickly, St Andrews University is proper jaw-dropping. Kings and queens get educated there. It's a bit Hogwartsy, but with modern bits bolted on. I was nervous, partly because it was a big event and partly because I'm not likely to become a king or queen. I guess there could be some sort of disaster that wipes out almost everyone in Scotland, and there's just me and my wife left. In which case, I'd vote myself in as King, but what I'm trying to say is that St Andrews is really posh and royal. And I'm basically not.

Remember, I'm the world's best worrier. That nagging little voice in my head that is full of self-doubt and criticism started shouting at me. I stood backstage, waiting to be introduced and rather stupidly, I dared to peep out from behind the curtain.

Bad move, Gav! The theatre was packed!

The voice in my head kicked off as follows ...

*Oh heck! Three hundred people! They're probably kings and queens, and I'm not even a prince. Guaranteed they're all a lot cleverer than me too. Oh my goodness, this is gonna go soooo badly.*

I tried to argue back against myself. It was like some sort of weird WWF Wrestle-Mania contest; me against me. I stood up to the bully in my head. *Shut up, inner critic. I am actually a lot cleverer than I look. And I eat pizza with a knife and fork which is pretty damn posh. And if there's an apocalypse and everyone's wiped out except me, I might be King of all Scotland. Plus, they invited me to come and do a talk, so shut up and get out of my head.*

But the inner voice came back at me. Real strong! It did that classic WWF thing where it slammed a chair across my head. *Yeah, they invited you to do a talk. Not a game of hide 'n' seek. Look around. It's 300 adults, in a theatre. There's nowhere to hide, idiot! You're doomed, Gav. You should get out while you can. Run. In fact, why don't you go and play hide 'n' seek? In one of the men's toilet cubicles. That way, nobody will see your embarrassment. Nobody will point and laugh and say, 'Look, there he is. He's the one who failed on stage....'*

Dear young reader, I was actually about to run and hide in the gents when I heard, 'Ladies and Gentlemen, please

put your hands together and welcome our first speaker,
Mr Gavin Oaaaaaaaaaaaattes.'

At that point I had no choice. Someone just pushed me on
stage. I kind of fell out there and stood, blinking into the
spotlight, while the polite applause died down.
'I'm going to do an experiment', I began. 'I'm challenging
you to a game of hide 'n' seek.'

There was a ripple of nervousness. In me yes, but more
so the auditorium!

'You all remember the rules from when you were a kid.

I'm going to shut my eyes and count to 10. And you're all
going to hide.'

I blinked some more and my throat went dry. 'The only
rule is that you're not allowed to leave the room. Got it?'
I closed my eyes, crossed my fingers and began; 'One...'

(to be continued)

# Un-worrying and un-tutting activity

If it's possible to 'worry yourself sick' then it must also be possible to 'un-worry yourself well'. So here's something we introduced in Brill Kid 1 that's well worth re-visiting.

Have you ever asked yourself: what hasn't happened that I didn't want that I haven't celebrated?

## Thought not!

Sadly, unless you're a black belt happiness ninja your mind doesn't sit in a boring English lesson thinking how lucky you are to have a teacher. As you trudge to school in the rain, your brain doesn't say 'Woohoo, all that lovely wet stuff will be watering my garden'.

Nope, your brain just tuts. And some brains get into the habit of tutting. In fact, some people grow up to be professional tutters.

So, to avoid getting into a tutting habit, it's worth training your noggin to do the opposite, which is to notice the many things that could have gone badly but didn't. Hence, what hasn't happened that you didn't want that you haven't celebrated?

That way, instead of a professional tutter, you become a professional celebrator. I woke up this morning and didn't have toothache. I had a shower and my leg didn't fall off, there wasn't a zebra in my Weetabix, my TV didn't blow up, my grandma isn't an alien, I haven't just stubbed my toe, I didn't accidentally turn up at school naked, my bottom hasn't turned green ....

All those bad things haven't happened to me today.

# WooHoo!

Of course, it's hard to notice something that didn't happen.

Have a go, it's fabulous fun. In fact, it's one of those mental muscles that gets stronger the more you exercise it. See if you can write your own list of bad stuff that hasn't happened that you haven't celebrated.

We'll get you started by doing number 1 for you...

1 _I haven't had my toes bitten off by a GIANT purple toad (called Frank)_

2 _____

3 _____

4 _____

5 _____

6 _____

7 _____

8 _____

9 _____

10 _____

frank →

# Things That Go Bump in the day

**BOO!**

Ghosts. They seem real but they're actually not. Big ones, small ones, friendly ones, cuddly ones, ones with chains, ones with sheets over their heads, ones made of marshmallows; none of them are real. Ditto monsters: Lock Ness, Yeti, vampires, werewolves, Godzilla ... it's imagination gone wild.

That's the 100% complete-and-utter truth. The top-and-bottom of it. Ghosts and monsters, they simply don't exist. It's a 99.9% true FACT.

Except the one in your wardrobe.

But ghosts not being real doesn't stop people from being scared of them. And being afraid of something is VERY real.

Fear is a funny thing (funny 'peculiar', not funny 'ha-ha'). For example, in the middle of the day, when your thinking is clear, worrying about the ghost that most definitely isn't hiding in your wardrobe seems silly. But when the lights go out, the ghost that still 100% isn't there becomes something to worry about. Worries about imaginary things get in the way surprisingly often and stop us from doing all sorts of things (not just looking under the bed or in the wardrobe). And not just at night. You could say there are things 'that go bump in the day' that we worry about, that we really shouldn't. This is a bit of a waste of time and energy, and can stop you thinking about more important things, like would you rather be covered in fur or scales, for instance. Or would you rather fight a mouse the size of a lion or a lion the size of a mouse?

Anyhow, while you're grappling with the lion/mouse thing, here's a list of seven 'Things that Go Bump in the Day' - common or garden everyday worries - 'daymares', and what to do about them.

## Daymare 1: Worrying about how you measure up to everyone else

Otherwise known as 'comparisonitis', this imaginary worry is never very far away. It follows us around, lurking just out of sight, waiting for an opportunity to raise its ugly head. We're very good at doing ourselves down. Rather than being proud of our achievements, we compare them with other people's and rapidly come to the conclusion that ours aren't really anything to be proud about.

Which is total nonsense, of course.

We tend to look at other people through rose-tinted spectacles and ourselves through a bug-splattered window screen.

Comparisonitis makes you green with envy. You compare your cleverness against everyone else's. Trainers, school bag, phone, holiday, hair, trousers, pencil case ... you even compare school dinners. You look at their lunch and it looks better than yours.

The modern world has made comparisonitis a lot worse. Things like social media and the vast array of TV channels means we now compare ourselves with everyone else on the entire planet. Celebs, billionaires, successful YouTubers, influencers, reality TV stars - we gawp at their lifestyles and want something similar.

It's hard to get your young head around the fact that these 'successful' people might not be as fantastically happy as you might think. Sure, when you watch them doing their thing they will probably look super-happy and confident, but true 'success' is when the camera's off. The quiet times. The alone times. The times that we don't get to see.

At Brill Kid HQ we believe that true 'success' is about how you feel about yourself. The problem with social media is that we end up comparing upwards to the land of airbrushed fakery.

So, just for a minute or two, let's have a go at comparing downwards. Again, it's hard to get your young head around the fact that if you're growing up in the UK, you'll be in the top 10% richest families on the planet. Yes! Even if you don't feel rich, we promise you've got an awful lot more than most of the other kids across the world. Assuming you've got a house, a bed, a school, some food, a tap with water, a loo and your family maybe has a car parked on the drive - you're doing better than most.

Let's compare and contrast with a kid of your age from a small town called Am Sac in the African country of Chad. It's a dusty outcrop of shacks on the southern edge of the Sahara Desert. Nobody owns a fridge. There are two taps, one at either end of the village. There is a school in the next town, about 8 miles away, but there's no bus so it's a 16-mile round trip on foot. There's no

*entire village does their business here. Imagine!*

Wi-Fi, Netflix, supermarket or warm shower. There's a row of four Portaloos where the entire village does their business.

Let's imagine we transported one of the children from Am Sac to your house for a day. What would their reaction be as you showed them around your house? Then you took them to your school, and, on the way home, you showed them the supermarket. That evening you had a family meal. They got to look in your kitchen cupboards at all the food and you introduced them to that big cold cupboard called a 'fridge'. Next you show them upstairs to your bedroom, with its comfy bed. That evening you introduced them to the internet, YouTube and you watched the Disney Channel on your iPad.

Our point isn't that your life is any better than theirs. Not really. Just like a celeb's life isn't any better than yours. Not really.

Almost everyone compares upwards. In comparison with a kid from Am Sac, your life is amazing!

*A steep upwards amazing!*

You have everything they ever dreamed of, and more.

You can only compare 'like' with 'like', which is another way of saying concentrate on doing your best every day, and make sure you like it. If you like what you do, chances are you'll like yourself and worry less about other people's opinions.

So, if you've got a bad case of comparisonitis, our top tip is to start comparing yourself with yourself. Ask yourself; *am I a slightly better human being than I was yesterday?* If you can answer 'yes' – honestly and consistently – other people will eventually struggle to match up to you.

That's a promise.

# Activity:
## Be the best for the world

Be the sort of child your mother, father, brother, sister, aunt, uncle, grandma, grandad, besties and next-door neighbour wants you to be. Which is ...

While you're at it, be the kind of learner your teacher wants you to be. Which is ...

And while you're in the mood, let's take it to the next level. You may as well be the kind of person *you* want to be. Which is ...

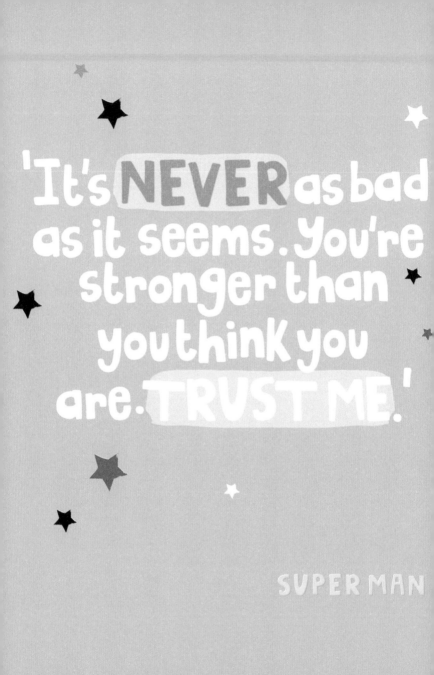

'It's **NEVER** as bad as it seems. You're stronger than you think you are. **TRUST ME**.'

SUPER MAN

Life's not fair. Why does bad stuff always happen to me? What's the point? The world's against me and btw everything's *booooooring!*

We rolled these five classic statements into one to get them out of the way.

The answers to the five are actually very simple:

1. Life's absolutely *not* fair, but then nobody ever said it was. Equally, the Am Sac village example shows that sometimes life's incredibly fair, but nobody ever says that.

2. Bad stuff absolutely does happen to you, just like it also happens to the other 7.5 billion runners and riders in the human race. Equally, good stuff also happens but most people never really notice. Being born and raised in a first-world country is the luckiest break you'll ever get. Take time to notice the good stuff. Live in a state of awe and wonder.

3. What's the point? The point is to *find* the point. If you can't see the point, it's not the point's fault. You need to look harder! Or look somewhere different. Or look within.

4. The world isn't actually against you. Or, indeed, for you. The world just does what the world does. And it pretty much always will.

5. For all those who think your day/life is *boooooring*, think again. You couldn't have got it more wrong if you'd tried. To make our point, please consider this tempting holiday offer:

Imagine, just for a moment, that we've invited you on an amazing 'holiday of a lifetime' trip into the solar system. You're going to spend the next 90 years cruising amongst the stars. In fact, let's upgrade the holiday ... let's go the long way and journey around the sun. The holiday is free and, in true game-show style, we'll throw in some spending money.

The big question is: would you go?

Ninety years is a long time, right? You're thinking that you'd miss your family, friends and cat. So let's upgrade you further. So that you're not lonely, you can take all your family and friends. Your cat/dog/guinea pig. Your house and, the clincher, we'll give you Wi-Fi.
You're probably thinking, there's a catch? You can't possibly be offering a lifetime of space travel, with family and friends. With Wi-Fi!

For FREE?

And, yes there is a catch. Welcome to earth. This is the journey you are already on.

welcome to earth

Your home is a ball of molten rock, spinning on its axis as it hurtles through space at 67,000 mph (thanks, Wiki). Around us are billions of other lumps of rock.

Earth travels all the way around the sun every single year. You already have friends, family and Wi-Fi. Maybe even some spending money too?

We really hope you're enjoying the adventure?

When you get a bit older, it's easy to forget that you're spinning through the solar system. You don't stop to admire the wonder of gravity that allows you to keep your feet planted onto this speeding bullet of rock. Most people never stop to consider that 100 metres beneath them is bubbling lava. We're standing on shifting tectonic plates that are slipping and sliding and banging into each other creating earthquakes. You can just plain forget that somehow life has evolved so that plants breathe out oxygen that we then guzzle into our human lungs. It slips your mind that the moon is in exactly the right place to affect the tides. Most people never think to remember that it's taken billions of years of human evolution to create us.

Look around. The people inhabiting planet earth right now are the result of generation *after generation after generation after generation after generation* ... after generation of human advancement.

YOU are the spearhead of human evolution. YOU are the sharp end. All the other human beings that ever lived, they existed to make YOU possible.

YOU are the very best that humanity can produce.

So, when it's a grey day, you're working on top-heavy fractions, and life seems a bit dull, it pays to remember that you're sitting on a spinning ball of molten rock, hurtling through the universe at 67,000 miles per hour. It's the only planet with fresh water, a breathable atmosphere, great music and guinea pigs.

And
guinea pigs!!

*How on earth is that 'boring'?*

'The universe is so big, it has no centre. We are the centre.'

Ms Marvel

## Daymare 3: Worrying about being perfect

Being perfect is nothing to purr about. So many people are on the look-out for perfection, but, of course, it's unobtainable. There's no such thing. Just like the Headless Horseman of Itchy Bottom, or the Ghost of Wilting Puddle, it doesn't actually exist. It's impossible to achieve perfection. Perfection means that something couldn't possibly be improved. With a bit more time, stuff can always be improved. But because we run out of time after about 100 years, we're limited on what we can achieve.

That doesn't stop you doing your best in the time you've got, though. Doing your best should be enough to satisfy you. No promises, but if you throw yourself into something, you're more likely to finish-up with the result you're after. Worrying about whether it's 'perfect' or not only makes it not so enjoyable.

Our advice? Quit trying to be perfect and start being awesome.

↖ Do that!

## Daymare 4: Worrying about losing your oomph

Here's a lovely word from an almost extinct language from France. *Startijen* is from the Breton language. It translates as your kick-start. When you're finding excuses instead of doing your homework, you need *startijen!*

Here's a top startijen hack; the 5-second rule. I read about it in a book by Mel Robbins and it's the simplest concept in the entire Brill Kid 2 book. Hands up if you can count backwards from 5 to 1?

*Excellent!*

In that case you'll love the 5-second rule. Let me explain by way of an example ...

Sometimes the alarm goes and I really don't feel like getting out of bed. Especially when it's dark outside and I have things to do that don't excite me. You'll be familiar with the feeling. It's easier to have a cheeky lie-in, an extra half an hour. But my extra 30 minutes in bed actually makes me feel a bit like the Hulk. I end up playing catch-up all day, rushed, stressed, on edge and angry with myself.

The 5-second rule has been astonishingly helpful. On those mornings when my mojo has slipped, instead of rolling over and going back to sleep I count down - 5, 4, 3, 2, 1 - and launch myself out of bed.

It works because your brain is very good at finding excuses for you NOT to do things. Whenever an event happens that requires you to take an action you know you should take, but don't want to, time begins to pass while you mull it over. Humans are the animal kingdom's best over-thinkers. The longer you leave it before taking action (the longer the gap of over-thinking time), the more likely it is that the gap gets filled with dread, anxiety, self-doubt and negativity or good old-fashioned things called EXCUSES. Those feelings settle in, get the better of you and you talk yourself into NOT doing whatever it is you could/should have been doing.

In my 'getting out of bed' example, if I think about it for too long my brain will come up with lots of reasons why staying in bed is the best option. It's so warm and snuggly in here and, besides, an extra half an hour won't hurt. In fact, it might do you good. And I can skip breakfast ... I mean, who needs breakfast anyway, it's so over-rated ... and before I know it, I've nodded off and I'm running late, hungry and stressed.

The 5-second rule cuts the thinking gap. The alarm goes and BOOM, 5 seconds later I'm out of bed and ready for action. Feet planted, sleep wiped from my eyes, I'm a readiness ninja. My brain is like 'Wow, no messin'. You mean ACTION, dude.'

> 'If watching is all you're gonna do, then you're gonna watch your life go by without ya.'
>
> Laverne,
> The Hunchback of Notre Dame

The 5-second rule is an accelerator, but it also works as a handbrake. It also stops you doing rubbish things.

- About to post a cruel message; 5, 4, 3, 2, 1 ... you've changed it to a nice message.

  About to guzzle a can of sugary fizz; 5, 4, 3, 2, 1 ... you've said 'Actually, can I have a fresh glass of milk instead, please?'
- About to open a packet of biscuits and scoff the lot; 5, 4, 3, 2, 1 ... you've reached for a piece of fruit instead.
- Listening to your friends saying horrible things about someone and about to join in; 5, 4, 3, 2, 1 ... 'Know what, most of the time she's a really nice person.'

The Bretons must be glowing with pride. Yes, their language is under threat but if it does disappear I do solemnly swear to keep *startijen* alive and kicking. The 5-second rule is *startijen* at its best. It's simple. It's free. It's quick. Best of all, the 5-second rule puts YOU in the driver's seat of your own life.

# Daymare 5: Worrying about whether the truth is true

Rhys age 10 | Rhys age 16

Rhys liked school. He enjoyed it. He was *someone*.

At the age of 10, he was the biggest in the year. He wasn't just tall, he was broad. He was one of those kids that grew and grew and grew until the age of 12, and then stopped. He didn't know it back then, but by the time he would finish his GCSEs at secondary school, he would be the shortest in the class. Funny, that.

At the age of 10, Rhys enjoyed being someone. If he was honest, he wasn't the best footballer, but that didn't stop him from getting the ball. He found he could lean on people and push them off the ball quite easily, or if he shouted at someone, they'd give him the ball. This worked quite well when he wasn't playing football, too.

He realised that he could get what he wanted simply by asking for it. And if he couldn't, he would take it, and no one ever really complained. Rhys liked getting what he wanted and liked getting his own way. He found that kids would laugh at his jokes when he made fun of people, even if it wasn't really funny. He liked getting a reaction. He liked being noticed.

His favourite way of getting noticed, getting a reaction and getting a laugh was to belittle others. 'Belittling' means to make small of other people. To make them be little. You can do this by making fun of their appearance, their accent, the things they like to do and even the things that they believe.

Rhys laughed at the children who went to worship on a Sunday. The others laughed, too. He laughed at the children who didn't go on Sunday, and the others would laugh, too. He laughed at what some of the kids had in their lunch box. He made fun of differences; different shoes, different accents, different colours and even the things that were really just the same.

But most of all, he laughed at the games the others played. He would sneer at the children battling imaginary orcs and goblins during playtimes, or the dancers pirouetting on imaginary stages. He poked fun at the explorers battling through imaginary jungles in search of long-lost treasures.

When a tooth fell-out and was placed in a special envelope to take home at the end of the day, Rhys would laugh loudest at those who believed the tooth fairy would stop by later. He didn't believe in magic and he didn't believe in fairies. Whenever Christmas came along, he even pretended not to believe in Santa.

He didn't believe.

He doubted those who dreamed.

He doubted those who played.

He doubted the stories that were told and the special times of year.

But most of all, Rhys doubted something even sadder.

He doubted himself.

Which was why he laughed at others when it was he who felt small. It was why he pushed them around when really, he wanted to be closer. It's why he laughed so loud when he felt so sad.

Rhys pretended more than the kids who played dinosaurs every break in the playground. He pretended he was happy.

You will have come across children like Rhys. They probably won't be called Rhys, but you'll know them all the same. You may even be that person. These are the people who make you feel not quite like yourself, even if you can't really put your finger on 'why'.

People believe all sorts of different things. Sometimes these are described as 'real' and sometimes they're imaginary. The truth is, there's an overlap between the two. Some things you believe others don't, and vice-versa. This means there isn't actually just one truth - there are lots of different truths.

Your truths are never fixed. They change as you change. You are never fixed. You grow. And so do your truths. Whatever size or shape they are, however, they are all equally valuable. Which means they must be valued equally - whoever they belong to.

Here's our top tips for handling Beliefs with care:

1. You may agree or disagree with someone. Your truths may be different and that's okay. Asking questions is always good, as long as you're ready to listen to the answer.

2. Always be proud of your beliefs. There will be times you might want to shout them from the rooftops and others when you would prefer to keep them to yourself. Experience will help you work out when is the right time to do this (or not).

3. You are allowed to be friends with people who have different beliefs to you or who don't believe. Everyone is different, which means anyone can fit in.

4. You can't borrow other people's beliefs. You can only believe your own. A belief is yours if it feels right. If it doesn't feel right, you can ask yourself a question, or someone that you trust. That often helps.

5. If you're not sure what to believe, it's okay. Sometimes things become clearer over time. You don't always have to make a decision if you're not ready to - your decision will eventually find you.

6. There will be things that you are absolutely 100% certain to be true that are not true. This is the same for absolutely everyone. Realising this is nothing to be embarrassed about - instead, it's something to be excited about. Like discovering a new flavour of ice-cream.

7. When you are absolutely convinced that you're right - and you *are* right - be kind to others who think differently. Don't judge and just accept. This is called humility.

8. There may be times when it's absolutely the right thing to do to stand-up for what you believe in. This is hard and requires bravery. Be kind to yourself if you can't find the bravery within you and be proud when you can.

9. Older people's beliefs are based upon their experience. This is quite useful - although probably gathered before you were even born. What was the case yesterday may not be the case tomorrow (or even today).

10. The belief that really matters is self-belief. Never doubt yourself. You are real. You are amazing. Believe in

# Bear-faced truth 1:

Polar bears can eat as many as 86 penguins in a single sitting. That's a lot of chocolate biscuits. No wonder they're fat!

# Bear-faced truth 2:

All polar bears are left-handed. Every single one of them. That's probably why you never see them with scissors.

To be clear, some things are absolutely worth your mental time and effort. The big issues listed above are reported on the news every day.

They have always existed and probably always will exist. #SadTruth.

In terms of these biggies, 'worry' is a waste of energy. The issues are so big that they're out of your control. They're out of any single person's control.

But they are issues that can be tackled collectively. So, if you feel passionately about any of them (or any other cause that we haven't listed) our advice is to put your energy into tackling the problem in a positive way. Get together with like-minded people and work on solutions. That's a good use of your energy. It's the opposite of worry. Worry drains you whereas finding positive solutions energises you.

You might not be able to change the world, but you can make a start by making a positive impact on your school or community. Channel your inner Greta. That way, one day it'll be you on the news, chatting about the difference you've made and you can be sure that we'll be watching, nodding and saluting your efforts.

## Daymare 7: Worrying that you're not enough

You are.

Even when you're feeling like you're not enough, you still are.

Not only are you enough, you are more than enough.

The world will try to make you think the opposite.

The world is wrong.

If you don't believe us, let's pick up where Gav left off. If you recall, he was standing onstage at St Andrews University for kings and queens, eyes closed, about to play hide 'n' seek, counting to 10 ...

I hadn't even got to two seconds and all I heard was 300 seats pinging up and 300 people hitting the floor, leaping to other seats, screaming, shoving, and laughing their heads off.

I stood there, eyes closed – *'three, four, five ...'* and, once again, my inner voice kicked in. My worrying had somehow shifted from 'nobody's going to play my stupid game' to 'oh my goodness, they're all playing my stupid game!'

I was so nervous, I nearly wee'd a little bit. 'Six, seven, eight ...'

I could still hear mad scrambling but as soon as I hit nine it went strangely quiet.

*'And ten ...'*

There was total silence except for one person who farted. It must have been the excitement.

In dramatically slow fashion, I opened my eyes. There

were squashed humans everywhere. Bodies were piled on top of bodies. Strangers on strangers! In row J there was a pair of legs standing upright. In row X there was a woman with a handbag in front of her face, which is the worst hiding place ever. There were people scrunched up in the aisles.

It was utterly brilliant!

My brain was buzzing with learning.

First, taking a risk had been worth it. I vowed to take a few more.

Second, I realised that if you give people the chance to play, most of them will take it. Think about it. We love to play. You do, I do, we all do. And if you don't love to play then you've never played properly. You've been doing it wrong. Or you've forgotten.

In that moment, I vowed to remember.

It's like when you want to go outside and build a den in the garden but someone else says, 'But it's going to rain in an hour.' Please don't ever become that person! In fact, be the opposite. Always be the person who wants to build the den, even in the rain.

We reckon loads of people the world over have forgotten how to play and what it actually feels like to be in that moment.

You're a kid. You're world class at playing. That's a superpower. Don't ever lose it.

Third, I realised I am whole. I am complete. I don't shout it out loud but I've learned to whisper it quietly in my head: *I am amazing!*

That nagging little inner critic who'd crashed a chair across my head had been talking absolute codswallop. If I'd have listened to my self-doubt I'd have been hiding in cubicle four in the gents' loo. I'd have missed this epic episode of my life. Hide 'n' seek with 300 adults would literally never have happened! From now on I was going to stand up against my shouty inner voice.

#IAmEnough

#YouAreEnough

#IAmAmazing

#YouAreAmazing

# Activity: Unleashing your ordinary everyday MAGIC

Harry Potter had a bad start in life. I'm imagining living under the stairs wasn't ideal. He had magical powers but he didn't realise until someone told him.

You're the same! Hopefully not the 'living under the stairs' bit but the magical everyday powers. So we're telling you. NOW. Before it's too late. It's unlikely you're going to be doing Lumos or Allohomora, but you've got the power of friendliness, kindness, happiness, smiling and positivity. You've got the power to be a nice human being and to make a difference to your teacher, classmates and at home. Some powers need a bit of work, like confidence, for example.

We want you to write 10 superpowers that you already possess and then create a Harry Potter type name for that power.

We'll give you two examples and then ask you to get your creative head on and produce the other eight ...

1. Kindness: 'Kind o amus'

2. A pleasure to have in class:
'Teacher Wowmundum'

3. _____

4. _____

5. _____

6. _____

7. _____

8. _____

9. _____

10. _____

Mary Mary quite contrary
How does your garden grow?

'Well, I plant some seeds.
Then I water them and sometimes I
have to put slug pellets out to stop them
eating the leaves. That's pretty much it?
There's a lot of waiting around.
It's not rocket science.'

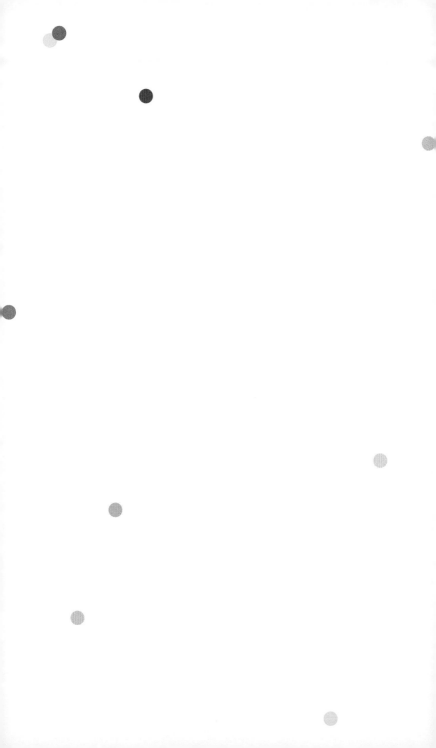

# dollop twelve:

## 'It'

3.4
Silliness Scale

When you're young, there's a fat chance that you don't know what you want to be when you grow up.

There's an equally podgy chance that when you've grown up, you still won't know what you want to do, even now that you're big.

Most books tell you to go for it. Dream big. Believe. Let nothing hold you back. Reach for the stars. That means most books are mostly true.

This isn't 'most books'. This is a Big Number 2, and in our book 'going for it' is all well and good, just so long as you know what 'it' is. Truthfully, at age 7 or 10 or 6 or 15 or 43, how many of us actually know, with certainty, what we actually want to do? And I'm talking 100% sure;

definite; there's-no-way-I'd-ever-change-my-mind, sure.

Very few of us.

Those of you who have already decided what you want to do with your lives might want to sit down for this next bit. It's easier to stand-up when you receive a shock sitting down than it is to sit-down when you receive a shock standing-up.

'You control your destiny. You don't need magic to do it. And there are no magical shortcuts to solving your problems.'

Merida (Brave)

Almost all of you who have already decided what you are going to do for the entirety of your lives, are wrong. That's right: *wrong*. So wrong that you have to pronounce the silent 'w'.

You're all *W-rong*.

You're not lying to yourselves - you're just being you, and therein lies the problem. The 'now' you is actually quite different to how the 'future' you will be. Yes, there will be the obvious differences (bigger bits, smaller bits, less hair, more hair) but the not-so-obvious-bits, too. Plus, the 'now' world is actually quite different to how the 'future' world will be.

That means there are a lot of unknowns coming your way. Some of the unknowns will be good, and some not so. The trick is to be prepared for a world of change so that whatever unknowns come your way, you can make the best of them. Embrace and make the most of the good unknowns and roll with the bad ones.

Finding out more about stuff that we know we don't know about is called 'prototyping'. It's what gets you thinking big – or at least, beyond the boundaries of what you know right now.

Exploring what's out there will help you to find your 'thing' and the thing about your 'thing' is that everybody's got one. Your 'thing' is something you enjoy and something that you're good at. You could call this a strength, dream, passion – whatever. If you can find your strength, dream, passion (whatever) and one day turn it into a job, you'll be one of the handful of humans who are totally happy at work.

The thing about your 'thing' is that it works even if you don't think you have one. If you've already decided that you absolutely haven't got a 'thing', that's your thing!

I've met adults whose absolute lack of get-up-and-go is their 'thing'. They've become super-expert at having no passion for life and that has become their life.

Obviously, we're encouraging you to aim a lot higher than that because there is an amazing life out there WITH YOUR NAME ON IT!

But to find your 'it' you have to do a bit of exploring. There's no big flashy neon signpost, with a giant finger lighting the way; 'HEY YOU! FOR AN AMAZING LIFE, TAKE THE NEXT LEFT TURN.'

Looking for your 'thing' means trying things out. No looky, no findy.

'Open different doors, you may find a you there that you never knew was yours. Anything can happen.'

Mary Poppins

Let's give you an idea of how prototyping works; how one thing leads to another thing and then to your eventual actual thing …

Imagine you like eating beans on toast. Beans on toast makes you smile. Prototyping suggests that whatever makes you smile is a good starting point. Scoffing beans on toast is your 'thing'.

← your thing!

Beans on toast

One day, instead of waiting for your dad to make beans on toast, you have a go at making your own. Extra yummy! So *making* beans on toast becomes your new thing.

You begin to experiment with toppings; cheese, brown sauce, Marmite, Weetabix, banana … and start posting pictures. Now posting pictures about weird and wonderful beans on toast recipes becomes your new thing.

One day, out of the blue, you shoot a short film comparing toppings - let's say honey versus ice-cream - and beans on toast film-making becomes your new thing.

Next day, mid-filming, your dog jumps up and grabs the toast from the toaster. You capture the footage, play it in slo-mo and it's epic so you start making home movies starring your dog. Your 'thing' has shape-shifted again.

It's such great fun that you spend your entire summer holidays perfecting your filming, editing and voiceover skills.

While shooting films with your mutt you discover that you really enjoy training your dog. In fact, you're really good at training your dog. Plus, all the other neighbourhood dogs you bring in as extras, they respond well to you too. Guess what? You're actually a really good dog trainer so that becomes your 'thing'.

Fifteen years later you're working in the police force as a dog handler, and absolutely loving it.

So, what started out as *eating* beans on toast, became *making* beans on toast, which became *experimenting with toppings*, which became *photography*, then *filming*, then making action movies with your dog, then *training your dog* and you eventually end up combining 'action movies', 'animals' and 'training' into a career in the police force.

You were experimenting all the way along. Trying stuff.

Giving things a go. Staying open minded.

*Prototyping.*

'So be sure when you step,
Step with care and great tact.
And remember that life's
A GREAT balancing act.
And will you succeed?
YES! you will, indeed!
(98 and 3/4 percent guaranteed)
Kid, you'll move mountains.'

Dr Seuss

The truth of the matter is many people don't try enough stuff. If you're not careful, you can get totally stuck at the 'eating beans on toast' stage. Obviously, that's fine if 'eating beans on toast' is your life's ambition. Finding your 'it', your x-factor, your passion - requires you to raise the bar.

We've put our heads together and collected some of our favourite rules that will help guide you through the next few years. Like we said, there is no bright flashing EPIC LIFE THIS WAY sign pointing the way, but this list is the next best thing.

Have a look. Maybe underline your Top 10 and most importantly of all, live by them. These rules will help you find your x-factor.

1. It's better to do something rather than nothing. Make life happen rather than let it happen.

2. Just because you might not be the 'best' at something doesn't mean it's not for you.

3. Just because you are the 'best' at something doesn't mean it is for you.

4. Parents want the best for you. They might not know what's best for you. They're still worth listening carefully to.

5. If you can't explain what it is you want to do, carry on looking until you can.

6. There is no time limit on deciding which path is for you.

7. You might change your mind and change your path.

8. You are allowed to change your 'thing'. In fact your 'thing' will almost certainly change.

9. The 'looking' is actually more important than the 'thing'. This is called living and is always the best thing to do with a life. Wherever it might take you.

10. We never really grow up, we only learn how to act in public.

11. You're never too old to learn something stupid.

12. Be a good friend. To yourself.

13. Live an interesting life. No one wants to talk to an old person with no stories to tell.

14. Knowledge minus Action equals Zero. In other words, if you know what to do, but do not do what you know, nothing happens.

15. No one's perfect, but everyone can be awesome.

16. Everyone seems normal until you get to know them.

17. 'Stressed', spelled backwards? Might that be the solution?

18. Those who complain the most tend to accomplish the least.

19. What you do every day matters more than what you do every once in a while.

20. Doing something and getting it wrong is at least 10 times more productive than doing nothing.

21. Kindness and hard work together will always carry you further than intelligence.

22. Lots of successful people have failed as many times as they have succeeded.

*True →*

23. It's always 'i' before 'e' except after 'Old MacDonald had a farm ...'.

24. If you're not feeling scared a lot you're probably not doing a lot.

25. Goals are important. But most people fail because they fail to set behaviours. Therefore, a good question is 'What kind of person do I need to be to achieve my goals?'

26. It doesn't matter what others are doing. It matters what you are doing.

27. The greatest mistake you can make in life is to continually be afraid you will make one.

28. Dreams, unlike eggs, don't hatch just by sitting on them.

29. When you stop chasing the wrong things you give the right things a chance to catch you.

30. Trying to be somebody you're not is a waste of the person you are.

31. Giving up doesn't always mean you're weak, sometimes it means you are strong enough and smart enough to let go.

32. Not getting what you want is sometimes a wonderful stroke of luck.

33. A harsh fact of life: Bad things do happen to good people.

34. No matter how many mistakes you make or how slow your progress, you are still way ahead of everyone who isn't trying.

35. Strive for progress, not perfection.

36. You can change your brain. Not change as in 'swap it for a better one', change as in 'shape and craft it into something amazing'.

craft it into Something amazing

Your brain

'There's room for everyone on the Nice List!'

Buddy the Elf

# Number 37

The next thing on our list of rules that will help you find your x-factor needs a bit of explaining, so here's number 37 in all its glory.

You've probably seen an Olympic Games?

These epic sporting events take place every 4 years. It's an exotic gathering where the best in the world take on the best in the world. It's great entertainment because they're all so fast or bouncy or throwy or bendy or stretchy or balancey or swimmey or rowey or jumpy or strong.

Ditto the Winter Olympics. Shooting headfirst down an icy hill on a baking tray - it's bonkers and brilliant at the same time.

The skill and talent on show is amazing. Which got us thinking, what if there was an Olympics for everyday things that require no skill or talent.

Absolutely none.

We're calling it the 'Everyday Olympics'. The clue is in the name. Rather than every 4 years, it happens every *single day* in an everyday town and it consists of 10 events that we can all take part in.

It's a decathlon. Here are our 10 everyday events that require zero skill or talent:

i. Working hard
ii. Smiling
iii. Having good manners
iv. Expressing gratitude
v. Doing extra
vi. Being prepared
vii. Having a positive attitude
viii. Being super-kind
ix. Showing up on time
x. Looking after your physical health

So our 37th point about finding your x-factor is to look in the mirror and ask yourself – with 100% honesty – if you were competing in these 10 everyday events, would you make the podium?

And with your hand on your heart, is there anything actually stopping you from going for gold?

Hence number 37; get the basics right. [7]

[7] From an original idea by the remarkable Paul 'Wolfie' Field

'I embraced who I am, and I don't want to stop'.

SUPERWOMAN

# Oh, and there's also a 38

It's probably worth summarising.

This dollop is about finding your x-factor - your 'it' - that certain something that lights you up. If you find it - which many people don't - it makes everything a whole lot easier because you begin to fall in love with life. So, we recommend that you experiment, try stuff, throw yourself into new opportunities, soak up the learning - because the more experiences you experience, the more likely it is that you'll find your 'thing'.

Then we did a massive long list of 36 tips that might help.

Then we added a 37th, which had an Olympic wrapper. It was about getting the basics right *every single day.*

But point number 38 can't be left un-said.

If you've never seen 'Kung Fu Panda'[8], treat yourself. It's an epic tale of martial arts, fitness, noodle soup and, erm, a rather podgy panda.

---

[8] Adapted from an original blog by the super-creative Nigel Percy

Here's the basic plot. Po, a buffoon of a Panda, trains to be a kung-fu ninja. Why? To earn the Dragon Scroll, which contains the secret that will enable him to fight the evil snow leopard.

With me so far?

Of course you're not. *It makes no sense whatsoever!*

But gosh, it's funny!

Meantime, back at the family cafe, his father (who is a bird, not a panda - stay with me, people!) reveals there is no secret ingredient in the best-selling 'secret ingredient' noodle soup. The cheeky bird has been fooling his customers for years!

Panda Po doesn't seem too bothered that his dad is a bird - a big fat liar of a bird - because he's too busy winning the Dragon Scroll. Which, if you remember, contains the secret of how to defeat the baddy leopard.

Po nervously unfurls the Dragon Scroll for the big reveal and - Ta-Daaaa - there are no words ...
... just a shiny reflective surface.

Po is looking back at himself.

At first he's horrified. He was expecting to find some answers but, of course, *he is the answer*. Po is already good enough, and BOOM, he knocks spots off that evil snow leopard.

Hoorah! From unfitness to fitness, unwellness to wellness, lack of confidence to total confidence, unfocused to focused, from buffoon to hero - in 95 minutes.

The village is saved, and we can do the whole thing again in KF Panda 2, and 3, and 4...

So here are two very important questions.
In fact, you could call them the Big Number 2:

a) Who's the most important person you talk to every day?

And ...

b) Who's the person in charge of your life?
Clue, put this book down, go to the bathroom and stand in front of your very own 'secret scroll', aka the 'bathroom mirror'.

*That* person will be there.

*That* person is in charge of your life.

*That* person is your x-factor.

*YOU* are *IT.*

**Congrats!** You've only gone and finished the entire book. So pop along to artofbrilliance.co.uk, download a Certificate of Brilliance, print it off, write your name on it and stick it on your bedroom wall. When you've had a bad day (which you sometimes will) the certificate acts as a big fat reminder of your awesomeness. Stand tall, salute the certificate and chant these words: 'Despite what the world's done to me today, I am amazing. Tomorrow I do solemnly swear to bounce back stronger.'

#wahoooooo!!!

get it NOW!!

**Certificate of Brilliance**

Congratulations on completing

BRILL KID The BIG number 2

May the AWESOMENESS be with you

*name*

*dates*

Read. Learn. Do.
PS, your training never stops

# the AUTHORS

## • ANDY COPE

Andy's got a bonkers life. He writes the world famous 'Spy Dog' stories and is also the UK's one and only Dr of Happiness. YES, that's an actual thing that you can be a doctor of! Who knew?

Dr Andy works all over the world delivering happiness and wellbeing workshops for businesses and schools. He's even been to Botswana. He's also written a shed load of teenage and adult books but you're probably not interested in that. He's got some pet pigs, is that interesting enough? He recently got badly stung by a jellyfish and had to have a bath in vinegar? That's proper interesting, right?

If you want to know more about Andy, check him out at www.artofbrilliance.co.uk, follow him on Twitter (beingbrilliant), Instagram (spydog451) or drop him an email at andy@artofbrilliance.co.uk.

## • GAVIN OATTES

Part child, part rock star, Gav is one of the best and silliest humans around. He runs a properly awesome company called 'Tree of Knowledge' whose purpose is to Inspire the World. And on a daily basis - within schools and businesses - that's exactly what they do. As part of this Gav and his team have worked directly with over 1,000,000 young people, empowering them to follow their dreams and be the best, kindest humans they can be.

He regularly does crazy things such as booking huge arenas and filling them with 12,000 people for MAHOOSIVE days of inspiration and learning.

If you want to know more about Gav and find out why companies such as NIKE book him to fire up their people, check him out at www.gavinoattes.com and/or www.treeof.com, follow him on Twitter (gavinoattes), Instagram (gavoattes), Facebook (Gavin Oattes) or drop him an email at gavin@gavinoattes.com.

## WILL HUSSEY

Will's real talent is rippling his tongue; that's right - like a snake. TRY IT. It's impossible. When he was 10, Will remembers his dad writing a book, which he thought was a pretty cool thing to do (even though it had absolutely nothing to do with snakes.) And neither does this, but **Diary of a Boa Constrictor** probably wouldn't make much sense ...'

## AMY BRADLEY

Amy is a FUN girl!

She has been drawing for as long as she can remember; it was her favourite thing to do as a kid and now, as a fully fledged adult, she reckons being an illustrator is the best job in the world!! Beat that hey!

She works out of her very own quirky studio in Uttoxeter, Staffs. Here, you'll never see her wearing shoes ... shoes totally cramp her creative style! And for when she really has to concentrate ... out comes the 'secret stash' ... chocolate, biscuits, cookies and 'Donut' worry; Donuts!! (Her all time fave!!).

If you wanna know more about Ames, then check out: www.amybradley.co.uk, follow her on Twitter: @amy_brad1 or even drop her an email: mail@amybradley.co.uk

# Index

Index

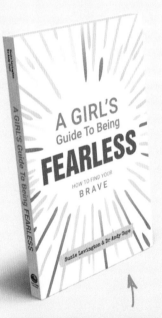